HBR Guide to
Thinking
Strategically

Harvard Business Review Guides

Arm yourself with the advice you need to succeed on the job, from the most trusted brand in business. Packed with how-to essentials from leading experts, the HBR Guides provide smart answers to your most pressing work challenges.

The titles include:

HBR Guide for Women at Work

HBR Guide to Being More Productive

HBR Guide to Better Business Writing

HBR Guide to Building Your Business Case

HBR Guide to Buying a Small Business

HBR Guide to Changing Your Career

HBR Guide to Coaching Employees

HBR Guide to Data Analytics Basics for Managers

HBR Guide to Delivering Effective Feedback

HBR Guide to Emotional Intelligence

HBR Guide to Finance Basics for Managers

HBR Guide to Getting the Right Work Done

HBR Guide to Leading Teams

HBR Guide to Making Every Meeting Matter

HBR Guide to Managing Stress at Work

HBR Guide to Managing Up and Across

HBR Guide to Negotiating

HBR Guide to Office Politics

HBR Guide to Persuasive Presentations

HBR Guide to Project Management

HBR Guide to
Thinking
Strategically

HARVARD BUSINESS REVIEW PRESS

Boston, Massachusetts

The web addresses referenced in this book were live and correct at the time of the book's publication but may be subject to change.

Library of Congress Cataloging-in-Publication Data

Title: HBR guide to thinking strategically.
Description: Boston, Massachusetts : Harvard Business Review Press, [2019] | Series: Harvard Business Review guides | Includes index.
Identifiers: LCCN 2018032610 (print) | LCCN 2018036095 (ebook) | ISBN 9781633696945 (ebook) | ISBN 9781633696938 (pbk.)
Subjects: LCSH: Strategic planning. | Business planning. | Industrial mangement.
Classification: LCC HD30.28 (ebook) | LCC HD30.28 .H394 2019 (print) | DDC 658.4/012—dc23
LC record available at https://lccn.loc.gov/2018032610

ISBN: 9781633696938
eISBN: 9781633696945

The paper used in this publication meets the requirements of the American National Standard for Permanence of Paper for Publications and Documents in Libraries and Archives Z39.48-1992.

What You'll Learn

Your boss just told you to "think strategically," but what does that mean? Acting on this feedback is crucial for anyone looking to advance their careers—especially aspiring leaders. But it rarely comes with concrete advice on how to do it.

At a basic level, thinking strategically means maintaining a broad perspective on every aspect of your daily work, from making decisions to setting your team's priorities and managing your own productivity. To do so, you need to understand your company's key objectives and strategy and keep those driving forces front of mind when you're faced with tough choices and competing goals. You must also align your team with these organizational needs, so that they're working on the projects and initiatives that contribute most to executing the company's strategy. And you must remain agile, able to identify changes in your business environment and alter course when objectives change.

It can be difficult to prioritize big-picture needs over short-term demands—and to know how to switch between the two. This guide provides practical tips and approaches to help you embed strategic thinking into your everyday work, so you can strike the right balance, create real value for your organization, be known as a strategic thinker—and achieve your own career goals.

You'll learn how to:

- Be more strategic in your daily work

- Ask questions to better understand your company's strategy

- Demonstrate your thinking skills in ways that your bosses will notice and respect

- Make faster, better decisions

- Identify when to broaden—or narrow—your perspective

- Detect patterns in internal and external trends

- Set your team's priorities based on goals, resources, and timing

- Navigate conflicting objectives and manage trade-offs

- Cut projects that are no longer adding value

- Communicate a company vision to your employees

- Align your team to execute the strategy

- Deal with common problems like unclear strategic goals or a strategy you disagree with

Contents

Contents

SECTION FOUR

Align Decisions with Strategic Objectives

Contents

SECTION SEVEN

Move from Thinking Strategically to Executing the Strategy

Contents

Why Everyone Needs to Think Strategically

You've just sat down with your boss to discuss your performance. You lay out all you've done in the past few years, highlighting your successes and contributions. You describe how you've effectively worked with your team, showing data about how they've met their goals consistently since you became their manager. You remind her that your past few performance reviews have been positive, and even note the additional work you've taken on to assist colleagues and even your boss herself. Then you make the ask: You'd like a promotion.

Adapted from *Pocket Mentor: Thinking Strategically* (product #13281), Harvard Business Press, 2010.

Your boss pauses for a moment, then replies, "You do good work, and you're a key member of the organization. There's no question your team benefits with you as their manager. But you're not quite ready to move up to the next level. Before we can consider you for a new position, you need to learn to think strategically."

Certainly, this is important feedback, and you have a vague notion of what it means: You're being asked to consider the big picture and make decisions with that larger view in mind. But this instruction rarely comes with concrete advice on how to do it. What does it mean to think strategically, and how do you develop that skill?

This book defines that term and shows the critical ways you can embed strategic thinking into your daily tasks, decision making, and management of others.

What Is Strategic Thinking?

As a manager, you routinely encounter complex situations, difficult problems, and challenging decisions. Your job is to deal with these situations as best you can by using the information you have. In an ideal world, you would have access to all the information you need to navigate through these situations and decisions. But in actuality, you probably only have a limited amount of information to work with. And because you sit in a particular part of your organization, you may have an incomplete view of the forces that lie outside your sphere of influence.

Strategic thinking helps you overcome these limitations. In its most basic sense, strategic thinking is about analyzing opportunities and problems from a broad perspective and understanding the potential impact your actions might have on the future of your organization, your team, or your bottom line. When you think strategically, you lift your head above your day-to-day work and consider the larger environment in which you're operating. You ask questions and challenge assumptions about how things operate in your company and industry. You gather complex, sometimes ambiguous data and interpret it, and you use the insights you've gained to make smart choices and select appropriate courses of action. You also make daily decisions about where you and your team spend your time, and you understand the trade-offs that come with those decisions.

By thinking this way, you ensure that every choice you make and every action you take drive results that matter. When you and others in your organization think strategically, you generate important benefits:

- You chart a course for your group that aligns with the overall corporate strategy and execute on it in your day-to-day work.

- You make smart long-term decisions that complement and align with decisions that others in your organization are making.

- You gain your employees' commitment to supporting your decisions.

- You boost your group's performance and maximize business results.

- You focus your daily work so you're working on priorities that make the highest contribution.

These benefits also yield valuable professional and personal benefits for you, including the respect and appreciation of your supervisor, peers, and direct reports—and perhaps that promotion you've been seeking.

Who Needs to Think Strategically?

At the most basic level, everyone should think strategically, so they are certain that the work they're doing directly contributes to the organization's strategic objectives and bottom line. As a manager, though, it's especially important to have this broader view, so you can ensure that your team's time and resources are aligned with the objectives that matter most and create the biggest impact for the company.

Strategic thinking is a particularly critical skill for ambitious managers who want to rise up the ranks of their organizations. Senior leaders may be the ones who set an organization's strategy, but you won't be promoted into these roles unless you can prove that you know how to think strategically on a regular basis first. Learning how to take the overarching needs and direction of the company into account as you prioritize objectives and manage trade-offs can help you transform from a manager into a strategic leader.

Your team should also learn to think strategically. By asking them the right questions and carefully planning their work, you can help them execute on strategic goals and increase productivity—and help to develop your workforce so when they're ready to become managers and leaders themselves, they have the critical skills they need.

Why Is Strategic Thinking So Hard?

One reason managers struggle to think strategically is because they feel they simply don't have the time. And certainly, when you're faced with immediate demands and deadlines, finding time to carefully consider your actions and decisions in light of strategic objectives can be difficult. But thinking strategically is more than allotting an hour or two per week on your calendar to consider the big picture. It plays a part in everything you do, from setting priorities for your team to planning your daily work to anticipating outcomes of everyday decisions.

And it takes a basic understanding of the organization's underlying purpose and strategy. But according to research by author and consultant William Schiemann, only 14% of organizations he surveyed claimed that their employees had a clear understanding of their company's strategy and direction, and only 24% felt the strategy was linked to their individual accountabilities and capabilities.[1] These statistics indicate a severe disconnect between our organizations' core objectives and what we *actually* do in our daily work.

It takes conscious effort to think strategically on a regular basis. You must actively ask questions and learn about your organization's key purpose and objectives. You must evaluate the pros and cons and potential repercussions of your decisions and your actions. You may need to let go of projects that your team has been working on for years in favor of new initiatives that could add more value. And in some cases, you may need to decline new opportunities, even if they seem exciting, simply because they are not in line with your priorities. You may be hesitant to make these tough choices, particularly as you face uncertainty and assess any risks associated with your final decision.

But you can overcome these challenges by learning the characteristics of a strategic thinker. Individuals who think strategically demonstrate specific personal traits, behaviors, and attitudes, some of which can seem to conflict. These attributes include:

- **Curiosity.** You're genuinely interested in what's going on in your unit, company, and industry and the wider business environment.

- **Consistency.** You strive to meet goals and pursue these objectives persistently.

- **Agility.** You're able to adapt approaches and shift ideas when new information suggests the need to do so.

- **Future focus.** You constantly consider how the conditions in which your group and company operate may change in the coming months and years. And you keep an eye out for opportunities that may prove valuable in the future—as well as threats that may be looming.

- **Outward focus.** You're able to identify trends and patterns in your industry and understand their implications. And you're willing to ask individuals outside your company for feedback to help you improve your business.

- **Openness.** You welcome new ideas from supervisors, peers, employees, and outside stakeholders such as customers, suppliers, and business partners.

- **Breadth.** You continually work to broaden your knowledge and experience so you can see connections and patterns across seemingly unrelated fields of knowledge.

- **Questioning.** You constantly ask yourself if you *should* be doing what you're doing—whether your team is focused on the right things, if there is something you can stop doing, if you should change your approach, and how what you are doing is creating value.

Adapting these qualities will help you "lift up" to consider the larger view, so you can continually ask yourself how your actions create value (or where they don't) for your company. By learning to do this regularly, you can maximize your contribution to your organization and set yourself up for growth.

What This Book Will Do

This guide provides you with a road map for developing your strategic thinking skills and using them to be a more effective manager and leader. The first section gets you started on this path with a picture of what it means to be a *strategic leader*—the characteristics you need to balance and the skills you need to learn. It includes an assessment to help you determine what your strategic thinking strengths are and where you need to improve, and it ends with advice on how to make sure your skills are noticed.

Once you understand these basics, you can move on to folding strategic thinking into your daily work and that of your team. We recommend six key elements for putting strategic thinking into action:

- **Understand your organization's overarching strategic objectives.** As an aspiring leader, you need to have a clear picture of the strategic goals your company is striving toward. Section Two describes how to ask the right questions about your company's strategy, assess risk, and identify your organization's impact on the world. You'll also learn how to build the right relationships to stay in touch with this strategic viewpoint.

- **Keep a big-picture perspective.** Section Three helps you avoid being bogged down by immediate, daily demands by showing you how to focus on the long term, keep strategy front of mind, and think more broadly about your organization's context. You'll learn how to make time to think about the big picture, see your company in new ways, consider the future in your daily actions, and observe internal and external trends to discover new connections and information.

- **Make decisions with the organization in mind.** Every choice you make should tie into your company's bottom line. Section Four helps you to reflect, rather than react, when facing difficult choices and problems, and provides a simple checklist to help you carefully consider your toughest decisions. And while data is crucial to decision making, the final chapter in this section provides a smarter, more strategic approach to using information to solve problems.

- **Set strategic priorities and manage trade-offs.** While you may have a clear understanding of your company's strategic goals, it's not always obvious how these translate into your daily work. Section Five provides a simple tool to help you sort critical, important, and desirable priorities. You'll learn how to create a plan to achieve these goals—and manage trade-offs when plans or projects change. And you'll learn how to decide what *not* to do— those initiatives that may need to be delayed or ended because other, more pressing objectives require your attention.

- **Align your team around organizational goals.** Finally, ensure that your team is working toward the needs of your company. Section Six provides questions and exercises to help your employees think strategically themselves and consider the future consequences of their own actions. You'll learn how to communicate with your team about strategy, particularly when the strategy changes.

- **Move beyond strategy and start to execute.** Strategy and execution are more closely inter- twined than many realize. In Section Seven, you'll learn how to execute more effectively by getting the right people working on the right problems and how to ask the necessary questions to narrow the gap between strategy and execution.

A final section focuses on navigating common problems of understanding and executing strategy—when the strategy is unclear or always changing, when you think the company strategy is wrong, or when your boss gives you conflicting messages. If any of these describe your situation, you can turn to Section Eight now.

This book is geared to help you change the way you think and to align your work and the work of your team with the larger objectives and purpose of your company. By thinking in this way, you'll have a better understanding not just of your organization, but of your industry as a whole, and you'll ensure that you're contributing to your company in the most valuable way possible.

Most of all, by reaping the organizational benefits of this work, you'll prove to yourself and others that you're ready to take on bigger roles and more responsibility—and get closer to that promotion you've been wanting.

NOTE

1. William A. Schiemann, "Aligning Performance Management with Organizational Strategy, Values, and Goals," in *Performance Management: Putting Research into Action*, eds. James W. Smither and Manuel London (San Francisco: Jossey-Bass, 2009).

Get Started: Be Strategic in Your Daily Work

CHAPTER 1

Strategic Leadership: The Essential Skills

by Paul J. H. Schoemaker, Steve Krupp, and Samantha Howland

The storied British banker and financier Nathan Rothschild noted that great fortunes are made when cannonballs fall in the harbor, not when violins play in the ballroom. Rothschild understood that <u>the more unpredictable the environment, the greater the opportunity</u>—if you have the leadership skills to capitalize on it. Through research at the Wharton School and at our consulting firm involving more than 20,000 executives

---

Reprinted from *Harvard Business Review*, January–February 2013 (product #R1301L).

to date, we have identified six skills that, when mastered and used in concert, allow leaders to think strategically and navigate the unknown effectively: the abilities to anticipate, challenge, interpret, decide, align, and learn. Each has received attention in the leadership literature, but usually in isolation and seldom in the special context of high stakes and deep uncertainty that can make or break both companies and careers. This article describes the six skills in detail. An adaptive strategic leader— someone who is both resolute and flexible, persistent in the face of setbacks but also able to react strategically to environmental shifts—has learned to apply all six at once.

Do you have the right networks to help you see opportunities before competitors do? Are you comfortable challenging your own and others' assumptions? Can you get a diverse group to buy in to a common vision? Do you learn from mistakes? By answering questions like these, you'll get a clear view of your abilities in each area. The self-test at this article's end (and the more detailed test available online) will help you gauge your strengths and weaknesses, address deficits, and optimize your full portfolio of leadership skills.

Let's look at each skill in turn.

Anticipate

Most organizations and leaders are poor at <u>detecting</u> ambiguous <u>threats and opportunities</u> on the periphery of their business. Coors executives, famously, were late seeing the trend toward low-carb beers. Lego management missed the electronic revolution in toys and gaming. Strategic leaders, in contrast, are constantly vigilant, honing their ability to anticipate by scanning the environment for signals of change.

We worked with a CEO named Mike who had built his reputation as a turnaround wizard in heavy manufacturing businesses. He was terrific at reacting to crises and fixing them. After he'd worked his magic in one particular crisis, Mike's company enjoyed a bump in growth, fueled in part by an up cycle. But after the cycle had peaked, demand abruptly softened, catching Mike off guard. More of the same in a down market wasn't going to work. Mike needed to consider various scenarios and gather better information from diverse sources in order to anticipate where his industry was headed.

We showed Mike and his team members how to pick up weak signals from both inside and outside the organization. They worked to develop broader networks and to take the perspective of customers, competitors, and partners. More alert to opportunities outside the core business, Mike and the team diversified their product portfolio and acquired a company in an adjacent market where demand was higher and less susceptible to boom-and-bust cycles.

To improve your ability to *anticipate*:

⊙ Talk to your customers, suppliers, and other partners to understand their challenges.

◔ Conduct market research and business simulations to understand competitors' perspectives, gauge their likely reactions to new initiatives or products, and predict potential disruptive offerings.

1) understand customer needs
2) Market & competitor Research

Scenario Modeling

- Use scenario planning to imagine various futures and prepare for the unexpected.

- Look at a fast-growing rival and examine actions it has taken that puzzle you.

Understand why losing customers

- List customers you have lost recently and try to figure out why.

- Attend conferences and events in other industries or functions.

Challenge

Strategic thinkers question the status quo. They challenge their own and others' assumptions and encourage divergent points of view. Only after careful reflection and examination of a problem through many lenses do they take decisive action. This requires patience, courage, and an open mind.

Consider Bob, a division president in an energy company we worked with, who was set in his ways and avoided risky or messy situations. When faced with a tough problem—for example, how to consolidate business units to streamline costs—he would gather all available information and retreat alone into his office. His solutions, although well thought out, were predictable and rarely innovative. In the consolidation case, he focused entirely on two similar and underperforming businesses rather than considering a bolder reorganization that would streamline activities across the entire division. When he needed outside advice, he turned to a few seasoned consultants in one trusted firm who suggested tried-and-true solutions instead of questioning basic industry assumptions.

Through coaching, we helped Bob learn how to invite different (even opposing) views to challenge his own thinking and that of his advisers. This was uncomfortable for him at first, but then he began to see that he could generate fresh solutions to stale problems and improve his strategic decision making. For the organizational streamlining, he even assigned a colleague to play devil's advocate—an approach that yielded a hybrid solution: Certain emerging market teams were allowed to keep their local HR and finance support for a transitional period while tapping the fully centralized model for IT and legal support.

To improve your ability to *challenge*:

- Focus on the root causes of a problem rather than the symptoms. Apply the "five whys" of Sakichi Toyoda, Toyota's founder. ("Product returns increased 5% this month." "Why?" "Because the product intermittently malfunctions." "Why?" And so on.)

  [handwritten annotation: — Find Root Causes Asking 5 "why"]

- List long-standing assumptions about an aspect of your business ("High switching costs prevent our customers from defecting") and ask a diverse group if they hold true.

- Encourage debate by holding "safe zone" meetings where open dialogue and conflict are expected and welcomed.

17

- Create a rotating position for the express purpose of questioning the status quo.

- Include naysayers in a decision process to surface challenges early.

- Capture input from people not directly affected by a decision who may have a good perspective on the repercussions.

(2) Interpret

Leaders who challenge in the right way invariably elicit complex and conflicting information. That's why the best ones are also able to interpret. Instead of reflexively seeing or hearing what you expect, you should synthesize all the input you have. You'll need to recognize patterns, push through ambiguity, and seek new insights. Finland's former president J. K. Paasikivi was fond of saying that wisdom begins by recognizing the facts and then "re-cognizing," or rethinking, them to expose their hidden implications.

Some years ago Liz, a U.S. food company CMO, was developing a marketing plan for the company's low-carb cake line. At the time, the Atkins diet was popular, and every food company had a low-carb strategy. But Liz noticed that none of the consumers she listened to were avoiding the company's snacks because they were on a low-carb diet. Rather, a fast-growing segment—people with diabetes—shunned them because they contained sugar. Liz thought her company might achieve higher sales if it began to serve diabetics rather than fickle dieters. Her ability to connect the dots ultimately led to a profitable change in product mix from low-carb to sugar-free cakes.

To improve your ability to *interpret*:

- When analyzing ambiguous data, list at least <u>three</u> <u>possible explanations</u> for what you're observing and invite perspectives from diverse stakeholders. *3 possible explanation*

- Force yourself to zoom in on the details and out to see the big picture.

- Actively <u>look for missing information</u> and evidence that <u>disconfirms your hypothesis.</u> *— Try to prove yourself wrong*

- Supplement observation with quantitative analysis. *— Rely on Data*

- Step away—go for a walk, look at art, put on non-traditional music, play ping-pong—to promote an open mind.

④ Decide

In uncertain times, decision makers may have to make tough calls with incomplete information, and often they must do so quickly. But strategic thinkers insist on multiple options at the outset and don't get prematurely locked into simplistic go/no-go choices. They don't shoot from the hip but <u>follow a disciplined process that balances rigor with speed, considers the trade-offs involved, and takes both short- and long-term goals into account.</u> In the end, strategic leaders must have the courage of their convictions—informed by a robust decision process.

Janet, an execution-oriented division president in a technology business, liked to make decisions quickly and keep the process simple. This worked well when the competitive landscape was familiar and the choices straightforward. Unfortunately for her, the industry was shifting rapidly as nontraditional competitors from Korea began seizing market share with lower-priced products.

Janet's instinct was to make a strategic acquisition in a low-cost geography—a yes-or-no proposition—to preserve the company's competitive pricing position and market share. As the plan's champion, she pushed for a rapid green light, but because capital was short, the CEO and the CFO resisted. Surprised by this, she gathered the principals involved in the decision and challenged them to come up with other options. The team elected to take a methodical approach and explored the possibility of a joint venture or a strategic alliance. On the basis of that analysis, Janet ultimately pursued an acquisition—but of a different company in a more strategic market.

To improve your ability to *decide*:

- Reframe binary decisions by explicitly asking your team, "What other options do we have?"

- Divide big decisions into pieces to understand component parts and better see unintended consequences.

- Tailor your decision criteria to long-term versus short-term projects.

- Let others know where you are in your decision process. Are you still seeking divergent ideas and debate, or are you moving toward closure and choice?

- Determine who needs to be directly involved and who can influence the success of your decision.

- Consider pilots or experiments instead of big bets, and make staged commitments.

⑤ Align

Strategic leaders must be adept at finding common ground and achieving buy-in from stakeholders who have disparate views and agendas. This requires active outreach. Success depends on proactive communication, trust building, and frequent engagement.

One executive we worked with, a chemical company president in charge of the Chinese market, was tireless in trying to expand his business. But he had difficulty getting support from colleagues elsewhere in the world. Frustrated that they didn't share his enthusiasm for opportunities in China, he plowed forward alone, further alienating them. A survey revealed that his colleagues didn't fully understand his strategy and thus hesitated to back him.

With our help, the president turned the situation around. He began to have regular face-to-face meetings with his fellow leaders in which he detailed his growth plans and solicited feedback, participation, and differing points of view. Gradually they began to see the benefits for their own functions and lines of business. With greater collaboration, sales increased, and the president came to see his colleagues as strategic partners rather than obstacles.

To improve your ability to *align*:

Over communicate

- Communicate early and often to combat the two most common complaints in organizations: "No one ever asked me" and "No one ever told me."

Align Key Stakeholders

- Identify key internal and external stakeholders, mapping their positions on your initiative and pinpointing any misalignment of interests. Look for hidden agendas and coalitions.

- Use structured and facilitated conversations to expose areas of misunderstanding or resistance.

- Reach out to resisters directly to understand their concerns and then address them.

- Be vigilant in monitoring stakeholders' positions during the rollout of your initiative or strategy.

- Recognize and otherwise reward colleagues who support team alignment.

(6) Learn

Strategic leaders are the focal point for organizational learning. They promote a culture of inquiry, and they search for the lessons in both successful and unsuccessful outcomes. They study failures—their own and their teams'—in an open, constructive way to find the hidden lessons.

A team of 40 senior leaders from a pharmaceutical company, including the CEO, took our Strategic Aptitude Self-Assessment and discovered that learning was their weakest collective area of leadership. At all levels of the company, it emerged, the tendency was to punish rather than learn from mistakes, which meant that leaders often went to great lengths to cover up their own.

The CEO realized that the culture had to change if the company was to become more innovative. Under his leadership, the team launched three initiatives: (1) a program to publicize stories about projects that initially failed but ultimately led to creative solutions; (2) a program to engage cross-divisional teams in novel experiments to solve customer problems—and then report the results regardless of outcome; and (3) an innovation tournament to generate new ideas from across the organization. Meanwhile, the CEO himself became more open in acknowledging his missteps. For example, he described to a group of high-potentials how his delay in selling a stalled legacy business unit had prevented the enterprise from acquiring a diagnostics company that would have expanded its market share. The lesson, he explained, was that he should more readily cut losses on underperforming investments. In time, the company culture shifted toward more shared learning and bolder innovation.

To improve your ability to *learn*:

- Institute after-action reviews, document lessons learned from major decisions or milestones (including the termination of a failing project), and broadly communicate the resulting insights.

- Reward managers who try something laudable but fail in terms of outcomes.

- Conduct annual learning audits to see where decisions and team interactions may have fallen short.

◌ Identify initiatives that are not producing as expected and examine the root causes.

- Create a culture in which inquiry is valued and mistakes are viewed as learning opportunities.

Becoming a strategic leader means identifying weaknesses in the six skills discussed above and correcting them. Our research shows that strength in one skill cannot easily compensate for a deficit in another, so it is important to methodically optimize all six abilities. The box "Are You a Strategic Leader?" at the end of this chapter contains a short version of our Strategic Aptitude Assessment (available online at hbrsurvey.decisionstrat.com), which can help reveal areas that require attention. For clearer and more useful results, take the longer survey and ask colleagues—or at least your manager—to review and comment on your answers.

***

Paul J. H. Schoemaker is the former Research Director of the Wharton School's Mack Institute and a coauthor of *Peripheral Vision* (Harvard Business School Press, 2006). He served as an adviser to the Good Judgment Project. **Steve Krupp** is Senior Managing Partner at Decision Strategies International, Inc. **Samantha Howland,** a Senior Managing Partner at DSI, leads its Executive and Leadership Development Practice.

ARE YOU A STRATEGIC LEADER?

As you complete this assessment, think about the work you have done over the past year related to developing new strategies, solving business challenges, and making complex decisions. Average your scores for each of the six leadership skills and then address your weakest area first, following the recommendations described in this article and online.

How often do you... RARELY **ALMOST ALWAYS**

Anticipate SURVEY AVERAGE: 4.99*

Gather information from a wide network of experts and sources both inside and outside your industry or function.

1	2	3	4	5	6	7

Predict competitors' potential moves and likely reactions to new initiatives or products.

1	2	3	4	5	6	7

Challenge SURVEY AVERAGE: 5.52

Reframe a problem from several angles to understand root causes.

1	2	3	4	5	6	7

Seek out diverse views to see multiple sides of an issue.

1	2	3	4	5	6	7

Interpret SURVEY AVERAGE: 5.78

Demonstrate curiosity and an open mind.

1	2	3	4	5	6	7

Test multiple working hypotheses with others before coming to conclusions.

1	2	3	4	5	6	7

(continued)

ARE YOU A STRATEGIC LEADER?

Decide
SURVEY AVERAGE: 4.81

Balance long-term investment for growth with short-term pressure for results.

| 1 | 2 | 3 | 4 | 5 | 6 | 7 |

Determine trade-offs, risks, and unintended consequences for customers and other stakeholders when making decisions.

| 1 | 2 | 3 | 4 | 5 | 6 | 7 |

Align
SURVEY AVERAGE: 5.01

Assess stakeholders' tolerance and motivation for change.

| 1 | 2 | 3 | 4 | 5 | 6 | 7 |

Pinpoint and address conflicting interests among stakeholders.

| 1 | 2 | 3 | 4 | 5 | 6 | 7 |

Learn
SURVEY AVERAGE: 4.95

Communicate stories about success and failure to promote institutional learning.

| 1 | 2 | 3 | 4 | 5 | 6 | 7 |

Course-correct on the basis of disconfirming evidence, even after a decision has been made.

| 1 | 2 | 3 | 4 | 5 | 6 | 7 |

*Averages are based on responses to this survey from more than 20,000 executives.

CHAPTER 2

To Be Strategic, Balance Agility and Consistency

by John Coleman

As a former consultant, I have a deep and abiding love for the use of 2 × 2 matrices in business strategy. My favorites are those that highlight two factors that seem, at first glance, in conflict. I find these particularly relevant to personal development, since individuals often must resolve the tensions between competing values and traits and must carefully monitor their own strengths so those strengths don't lapse into weaknesses.

Adapted from "The Best Strategic Leaders Balance Agility and Consistency" on hbr.org, January 4, 2017 (product #H03DD0).

I've recently been thinking about this with regard to how leaders, and those aspiring to leadership positions, can be more strategic—able to effectively execute the core of their business while remaining open to trends in the market and adapting to meet them. I've begun to view this as the ability to hold two specific traits in balance: consistency and agility. Figure 2-1 illustrates these qualities in such a matrix.

The best performers are, of course, *consistent*. Consistent leaders work hard and show up on time. They set goals for themselves and their employees—and they achieve them. They plan diligently and produce excellent products and experiences for clients time and time again. They possess resilience and grit. Consumers expect consistent products; people appreciate consistent management.

But if organizational leaders are merely consistent, they risk rigidity. In changing environments, they can struggle to adapt and may cling to old habits and practices until those practices become counterproductive, distracting them from the more important new work that needs to be done.

On the other side of the spectrum, great leaders are *agile*. Markets demand that companies and people adapt and change constantly. According to one analysis by Mark J. Perry at the American Enterprise Institute, 88% of companies appearing on the *Fortune* 500 list in 1955 were not on it in 2014 (having merged, gone bankrupt, or fallen off the list).[1] As we know, buggy-whip makers and telegraph companies must evolve or die. And the most successful managers must change similarly as they

FIGURE 2-1

Strategic leaders must be agile and consistent at the same time

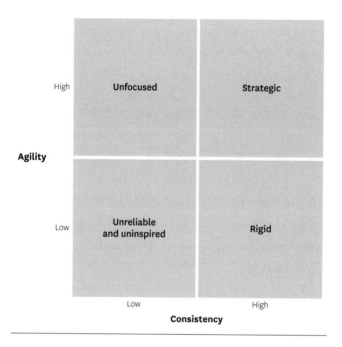

assume additional or different responsibilities through their careers, moving from head of sales to COO or from CFO to CEO. These leaders must pivot when needed, and agility requires that they be intellectually curious, ready to learn from others, communicative, collaborative, and willing to change.

But just as consistency can become rigidity, agility can become a lack of focus when it isn't tempered by consistency. Purely agile leaders may be visionaries and change agents but they lack the single-mindedness and dedication to execute their visions. They often turn to new projects before they've finished ongoing projects, and, in extreme cases, force their teams or organizations into chaos and instability.

It's in the combination of consistency and agility that leaders can become strategic, performing an organization's purpose with excellence but changing course when the situation demands. These leaders have high standards, achieve goals, and expect consistency, but they are also open to change, keep an eye on the external environment, and understand when old ways of working no longer pass muster in the market in which they compete. They stay the course until it no longer makes sense and combine continuous improvement with ideation and strategy.

Of course, few individuals are equally consistent and agile, just as few people are ambidextrous. So how can you hold these traits in balance?

First, as Socrates said, "Know thyself." Are you more prone to consistency or agility? Are you more naturally capable of deep focus or ideation? Do you thrive in situations of chaos and rapid change or in periods that require relentless pursuit of a clearly defined goal? If in doubt, ask a spouse, best friend, or close work colleague—they almost always know. Understanding and accepting our tendencies is the foundation for growth.

With that understanding in hand, surround yourself with others who complement your traits. For managers, it's wise to find a strong "number two" who can check your worst impulses and enhance your strengths. Are you an agile visionary? Find a structured, methodical, and disciplined deputy or peer. If you are a consistent operator, find a strong voice for agility on your immediate team or a mentor to push your creativity, no matter how frustrating that might be. And empower those people to speak up and challenge you.

Support this organization model with operational process. To ensure consistency, develop strong dashboards and balanced scorecards to assure outcomes are regularly reached and continually improving. To assure agility, develop a fluid planning model that allows the organization to change outside of the formal annual planning process and create an annual strategic planning process that looks outward to the external environment and forces the organization to contemplate big ideas. As an individual, do this for yourself, perhaps as an end-of-year exercise, to make sure you're pointed at the right goals and aspirations for where you are as a leader.

Finally, with these people and processes in place, seek to learn and grow. If you're naturally an agile thinker, you may never be the most consistent operational manager, but you can get better. And you can often do so simply by consciously observing what's working around you and then forcing yourself to expand your skills in that direction. Make note of those traits you admire in others—those that complement your own—and find ways to practice them.

As an aspiring leader, you must know how to balance consistency and agility in your career and in the organization you serve. Are you doing so today? If not, take steps to understand yourself and think about the people and processes around you that can help move you into greater balance.

———————

John Coleman is a coauthor of the book *Passion and Purpose: Stories from the Best and Brightest Young Business Leaders* (Harvard Business Review Press, 2012). Follow him on Twitter @johnwcoleman.

NOTE

1. Mark J. Perry, "*Fortune* 500 Firms in 1955 vs. 2014; 88% Are Gone, and We're All Better Off Because of That Dynamic 'Creative Destruction,'" aei.org, August 18, 2014, https://www.aei.org/publication/fortune-500-firms-in-1955-vs-2014–89-are-gone-and-were-all-better-off-because-of-that-dynamic-creative-destruction/.

CHAPTER 3

Prove You're Ready for the Next Level by Showing Off Your Strategic Thinking Skills

by Nina A. Bowman

One of the cardinal rules for securing a promotion is that you already need to be demonstrating many of the skills required at the next level. Emerging leaders must achieve results and manage resources and people well, but the most effective, "ready to be promoted" managers also display another critical skill—the ability to think strategically.

Showing strategic thinking skills tells your bosses that you're able to think for yourself and make decisions that position the organization for the future. It assures them that you aren't making decisions in a vacuum but are considering how other departments might be affected or how the outside world will respond.

We all know that developing strategic thinking skills is important, but many don't realize how critical *showing* these skills to your boss and other senior leaders is to your career advancement. To really stand out, you have to both develop *and* demonstrate them.

- *Developing* great strategic thinking skills is a demanding challenge. It requires you gain exposure to strategic roles, synthesize broad information, participate in a culture of curiosity, and gather experiences that allow you to identify patterns and connect the dots in novel ways. That's why high-potential and leadership development programs often include job rotations, cross-functional projects, and face time with senior leadership—all of these accelerate the development of strategic thinking.

- *Demonstrating* strategic thinking, on the other hand, requires that you are simultaneously a marketer, a salesperson, and a change agent. You may be able to show your skills immediately and start to stand out today. Proactive and widespread communication of your strategic efforts combined with the courage to challenge others and initiate and drive your strategic ideas are what make your boss and peers take notice.

The case of one of my coaching clients illustrates the distinctions between developing and demonstrating strategic skills.

"Not Strategic Enough"

Tim Waters (not his real name), vice president of the U.S. supply chain for a growing medical products company, hoped to be named global senior vice president of supply chain but sensed that his promotion discussions were stalled. Tim had a good reputation for responding to business unit leads, and he worked tirelessly and effectively to keep the supply chain functioning well. He was therefore surprised to receive informal feedback from the head of HR, a longtime colleague and friend, who said that a few influential executives had voiced concern that Tim "wasn't strategic enough." These executives felt Tim was good at keeping the trains running, but he had not driven proactive change in the organization or set a strategic vision for supply chain. Tim agreed that strategic thinking could be an area of personal growth and decided to engage an executive coach to help him hone and demonstrate these skills.

Developing Strategic Thinking

Build a solid foundation of trends and insights

Any manager's first step toward developing strategic thinking skills is learning more about what's happening beyond their day-to-day work. By better understanding trends within the function, the company, the industry, or the macro environment, and asking, "How might this impact my function or organization?" new managers and seasoned managers alike can make thoughtful strategic suggestions.

Tim had over 20 years of experience in supply chain but had stopped attending industry conferences and engaging with his external network of analysts and supply chain peers due to time pressures. He knew, honestly, that he had been coasting lately, operating as if he already knew everything that he needed. His first concrete step was to recommit to updating his knowledge by reading relevant articles, getting outside his organization routinely, and reconnecting with external contacts. Tim quickly learned about the new ways in which peer companies were addressing challenges. He felt energized by this new knowledge and quickly saw himself developing sharper views on ideas for his own company and asking better strategic questions.

Prioritize strategic thinking

Finding time to plan, think, and stay up to date is challenging for managers at all levels. Strategic thinking is a textbook example of an "important, not urgent" activity that tends to get pushed aside by the day-to-day. It requires discipline to carve out dedicated time for learning and deliberate thought, and young managers in particular should build habits early to ingrain this mindset.

Tim realized that his packed schedule was keeping him from ongoing learning and reflection. Changing how executives perceived him was a long-term goal, so he knew that he needed to develop practical, sustainable processes to keep himself and his team up to date on trends. Without routines, urgent demands would always crowd out the need to look ahead.

Tim committed himself to attending two key events a year and blocked them off on his calendar before it got filled with other meetings. He set aside 30 minutes a week to read relevant articles and to connect with external resources. He made the discussion of new ideas a recurring agenda item in the weekly team meetings he ran and asked team members to take turns bringing in a provocative article. Tim realized that good ideas can come from anyone, and that developing the strategic thinking skills of his direct reports would accrue to his benefit as well.

Lastly, Tim instructed his assistant to block out 30 minutes on his calendar before important meetings. He knew that barely having time to collect his thoughts before going into meetings made him unprepared, less vocal, and certainly less willing to challenge other's ideas. Just a half hour, once or twice a week, would allow him to begin to shape his point of view on important issues and identify a few strategic questions to bring up.

Demonstrating Strategic Thinking

Bring a point of view to the table

To display strategic thinking, you must synthesize disparate thoughts into a point of view and a vision that your bosses can see. You don't want to be the manager and leader who, lacking confidence in your own vision, tries to hedge by staying quiet or deferring to the most senior person in the room. While being politically astute is important, your leaders want to know what you think, and they view your worthiness for promotion through the lens of how ready you are to make bigger decisions. By asking yourself, "Do people know where I stand?" before meetings, you can sharpen your ability to demonstrate this strategic skill.

Tim's efforts to shape his ideas began to pay off over time. New thoughts emerged, and Tim was able to shift his contributions in senior executive meetings from operational input to strategic input. He took time to package his ideas into a vision for the organization and engaged his peers in new discussions about how the vision could impact their areas. Some conversations went better than others, and Tim quickly learned how to frame his thoughts in a way that was not threatening to his peers.

Having greater clarity of vision also enhanced Tim's effectiveness as a supervisor. Tim was able to see how his team was missing the specific skills needed to support the vision. Now, instead of having reactive discussions with his HR business partner, he was able to engage in forward-looking discussions about strategic hiring and leadership development opportunities for his team. Demonstrating that you think strategically about hiring and talent development is a surefire way to make your leaders notice you.

Show that you can initiate innovation and bring strategic change

To be viewed as a strategic thinker, it is critical to go beyond offering ideas and showing understanding outside your area: You must also demonstrate that you can use your knowledge to put new ideas into action. The scope of such an initiative will depend on your role. But no matter your level, you can demonstrate strategic thinking by executing an innovative project that shows that your understanding extends beyond your current function and making your efforts visible to others.

Tim channeled the new energy and vision he had gained into a strategic planning process that culminated in formal recommendations for the supply chain group. Tim communicated the project and its milestones across the organization, allowing the executive team to see that he could lead a strategic initiative; previously, Tim would have kept it behind the scenes. Boldly suggesting value-added changes was a welcome shift to both Tim and his colleagues. Tim felt he had greater control, projecting greater confidence because he was no longer just reacting to others' suggestions and issues, and Tim's colleagues also appreciated that he was initiating improvements without their prodding.

Tim's journey to demonstrating strategic thinking took him longer than he had expected, but over time, his boss, peers, and team noticed the changes and viewed them positively. Tim was promoted to the global role a year later and was ultimately better equipped to navigate the bigger job.

The need to develop strategic thinking, and making sure your bosses can see it, is universal. You can start small and begin your journey by practicing the individual skills involved. If you are a functional worker, you might begin by attending a conference or by raising your hand to assist on a interdepartmental initiative. You can gain practice with developing a point of view by making a list of strategic questions before entering meetings. As a new manager, you might focus on building your network outside of your department or addressing pain points within your own department. If you are not sure where to start, the rest of this guide provides many practical suggestions that will allow you to build your strategic thinking skills one step at a time.

Nina A. Bowman is a Managing Partner at Paravis Partners, an executive coaching and leadership development firm. Previously, she held various advisory and leadership roles in strategy. She is an executive coach and speaker on issues of strategic leadership, leadership presence, and interpersonal effectiveness. She is also a contributing author to the *HBR Guide to Coaching Employees* (Harvard Business Review Press, 2015).

Understand Your Organization's Strategy

CHAPTER 4

Understanding Your Organization's Strategy

Your organization has an overarching plan for developing its competitive advantage, likely served by a series of cascading goals for business units and individuals. As a manager, you work through your employees to support the company's overall plan; your own strategies and goals must align with the priorities set from above.

But before you can align your work with a larger strategy, you need to know what that strategy is. Simply reading a strategy memo isn't enough. You must actively work to clarify what are you're supposed to be delivering

Adapted from *Harvard Business Review Manager's Handbook* (product #10004), Harvard Business Review Press, 2017; *Harvard Business Essentials: Manager's Toolkit* (product #2896), Harvard Business School Press, 2004; and "Worksheet for Clarifying Strategic Objectives," *New Leader Program*, Harvard Business Publishing, 2016.

and how you're supposed to do it—by clearly understanding your company's strategic vision and goals, and
assessing potential risks.

Step 1: Gather Information About Strategic Objectives

Review any strategy documentation that your team, division, or organization may have. This information will
be vital to understanding what targets the company aims
to meet and how leadership teams are communicating
this direction. But don't stop there. Set up a "listening
tour"—a series of conversations with key figures in your
company that will help you clarify its strategic objectives.
It's obviously important to interview your boss, but you'll
want to understand the perspectives of other leaders in
your group or organization as well.

Don't just look up for answers. Consider coworkers
below or lateral to you. You also want to hear from people with insight who may not have positional power to
act on their ideas, but will have a good read on what's
really going on. Who's been at the company for a long
time? Who's worked closely with the current leadership?
Who recently transferred from a company that went
through a similar change process? For example, a peer in
R&D might have niche knowledge about how technology
in your field is likely to evolve, while someone in market research may have the most up-to-date information
about how your customer base is evolving. (Use the sample language in the box "Defining Strategic Objectives"
as a template for these discussions.)

DEFINING STRATEGIC OBJECTIVES

Your Organization

- "What are the company's major strategic objectives right now?"

- "What are the major needs/challenges/opportunities we're facing over the next six months? Year? In the long term?"

- "I'm hearing that _____ is our primary priority right now, and that long-term we're preparing for _____. Am I reading the landscape right? What am I missing?"

Your Team

- "How do you see my team fitting into this picture?"

- "What are your top priorities for my group? What are the big needs/challenges/opportunities you'd like to see us tackle in the next six months? Year? In the long term?"

- "I'd like to see my team do _____ and _____. What are your thoughts?"

You

- "What role would you like to see me play in carrying out this strategy?"

(continued)

DEFINING STRATEGIC OBJECTIVES

- "What are the major needs/challenges/opportunities you'd like to see me take on in the next six months? Year? In the long term?"

- "I think I'd be most useful doing _____ and _____. What are your thoughts?"

- (With your boss or key peers) "What are your major objectives right now within the organization? How can I support them?"

As you conduct these conversations, press for clarity and specificity. Ask questions such as, "I hear you saying that innovation is a priority for my team. Where would you like to see us focus?" If open-ended questions aren't getting you answers, offer limited choices: "I think there's a lot of opportunity to innovate with the way we conduct client relations and with our inventory technology. Where would you like us to focus?"

Reflecting on your conversations, note the gaps and contradictions in what you're hearing. Do different people emphasize different strategic goals? Is your supervisor tasking you with projects that don't match the priorities they've defined? If you can, press to figure out where these inconsistencies are coming from: "How do you see this special assignment supporting the overall direction you've sketched for my department?"

Step 2: Analyze Risk in Strategic Objectives

Once you've identified the goals and opportunities in front of you, review all the information you've gathered and ask where the biggest risks are:

- What are the major sources of uncertainty in your team's future?

- What external risks can you identify? Think about categories like funding; competition and conflict with other units in the company; the status of your patrons or protectors within the company; and potential reorganization.

- What internal risks can you identify? Consider upcoming personnel changes, team dynamics, and office politics.

Filter everything you're learning through a more personal question, as well: What will it take for you to be successful in your role? This isn't vanity on your part. Your bosses expect you to be a strategic thinker, and that means learning to evaluate the risks and opportunities that you must navigate yourself.

Ask yourself these questions:

- What are the major sources of uncertainty in my own future?

- What are professional risks to my success? Think about categories like your professional goals; your experience, training, and accreditation; your network, especially within your company; and work logistics (for example, a difficult commute).

- What are personal risks to my success? Think about your health, your family, your finances, and your personality and disposition.

Once you understand the major risks to your success, analyze them from a few different angles. First, which of these risks are most likely to have a direct impact on your success? What do you absolutely need to plan for? For example, if you know that your workload makes it hard to meet important deadlines—say, submitting legal filings to a court—you must find a strategy for dealing with this problem.

Second, which risks are impossible or impractical to counter? What can't you plan for? For instance, you may not know if your company or division may be sold in the coming year, but if you haven't seen any indications that this will happen, it may not be worth planning for. You can compensate for this risk by solving a related problem—say, planning for delays or creating new ways to strengthen relationships with other team members.

Third, which are easy to plan for? Are there high-value actions that would be easy for you to take? If your inexperience with a particular coding language compromises your ability to lead a new product rollout, for example, find out if your company will pay for you to take a course in the language or bring an expert in from outside the company.

Finally, who else in your organization do these risks touch? Who can be a strategic ally? Perhaps if your team needs expanded IT support to meet its performance targets, you might look for another unit in the company that's also underserved to help you press for more resources.

Understanding your company's strategy is crucial to ensuring that your work and the work of your team align with overarching priorities. By asking the right questions of key individuals in your organization and assessing the risk associated with these objectives, you can get a fuller picture of what your company strives to do and take steps toward this strategic direction.

CHAPTER 5

Strategy Isn't What You Say, It's What You Do

by Roger L. Martin

You sometimes hear managers complain that their organization has no strategy. This isn't true. Every organization has a strategy: *Its strategy is what it does*. Think about it. Every organization competes in a particular place, in a particular way, and with a set of capabilities and management systems—all of which are the result of choices that people in the organization have made and are making every day.

When managers complain that their company's strategy is ineffectual or nonexistent, it's often because

---

Adapted from "Strategy Isn't What You Say, It's What You Do" on hbr.org, June 18, 2014 (product #H00UXA).

they haven't quite realized that their strategy is what they're doing rather than what their bosses are saying. In nine cases out of ten, the company will have an ambitious "strategy statement" or mission of some kind: "We are going to be the best in the world in our industry and always lead innovation to the benefit of all of our customers."

The bosses will have worked hard to come up with such a statement, and it may very well be a praiseworthy one. But unless it is reflected in the actions of an organization, it is not the organization's strategy. A company's strategy is what the company's people are actually doing, not the slogan their bosses articulate.

The point is that everyone needs to connect the dots. If strategy is what people do rather than what bosses say, it is absolutely critical that each person in the organization knows what it means to take actions that are consistent with the intent of the strategy as asserted.

Strategic choice-making cascades down the entire organization, from top to bottom. This means that every person in the company has a key role to play in making strategy. Performing that role well means thinking hard about four things:

1. What is the strategic intent of the leaders of the level above mine?

2. What are the key choices that I make in my jurisdiction?

3. With what strategic logic can I align those choices with those above me?

4. How can I communicate the logic of my strategy choices to those who report to me?

If you as a manager can do the first three of these four, then you will own your choices and own your strategy. If you do the fourth, you will set up your subordinates to repeat these four things and thereby own their choices and their strategy, and pass on the task to the next layer of the company. If each successive layer assumes this level of ownership, the organization can make its bosses' statement a real strategy rather than an empty slogan.

———————

Roger L. Martin is a professor at and the former Dean of the Rotman School of Management at the University of Toronto. He is a coauthor of *Playing to Win* (Harvard Business Review Press, 2013).

CHAPTER 6

Building a Strategic Network

by Linda A. Hill and Kent Lineback

We all know how important networks are in all the different parts of our lives: medical and health, financial and legal, and especially in work and career. What many don't know is that to be successful as a manager and leader, you need not one but three networks: operational, developmental, and strategic.

First, of course, is the network of those you and your group need to do your day-to-day work. These are people in other units of the company, and outside, on whom and on whose work you rely on do your work. This is your *operational network*. Those in it don't work for you, but

---

Adapted from "The Three Networks You Need" on hbr.org, March 3, 2011 (product #H006X5).

your success depends on them. It also includes those who rely on you and your group to do *their* work. Though you may not need them, their demands on you can have a big impact on how you spend your time and attention.

Your *developmental network* is the collection of individuals whom you trust and to whom you can turn for a sympathetic ear, advice (depending on their experience), and a place to discuss and explore professional options. One way or another, these are people who help you grow as a manager and leader.

You create both operational and developmental networks naturally. The people in your operational network are those you must work with every day. And most of us naturally turn to knowledgeable friends and acquaintances for personal help with professional dilemmas. You may not have thought about these two groups as networks, but they are. In our experience, most managers spend too little time and care on building and maintaining them. They're mostly forged by immediate need and happenstance, and they often lack key people. But most managers create them, if only in rudimentary form.

The third network you need, your *strategic network*, is the one many managers don't create at all because it doesn't naturally evolve in the everyday course of work and life. A strategic network is about *tomorrow*. It comprises those who can help you do two critical tasks: first, define what the future will bring, and second, prepare for and succeed in that future. There will be some overlap between this network and your operational network, but the differences are likely to be significant, too.

Nobody can predict the future, but that doesn't mean you don't need to worry about it. Even if you can't know what's coming, you still need to identify what *might* happen—the most probable futures that lie ahead—and think about how you might prepare for them. You need a strategic network because the forces that drive change in your field will probably come from outside your current world. That means you need some way to discern those forces when they first appear on or over the horizon, not when they arrive at your door. That's the purpose of this network.

Your strategic network consists of outposts—individuals who work on the horizon of your world and can see into worlds beyond, both inside and outside your organization. Because there are many worlds surrounding yours and you can't predict which will produce the invading forces of disruption, you need several outposts—and you need to create them intentionally, because such relationships won't develop naturally. That's the tough part.

The good news is that your links to these outposts will mostly be what sociologists call "weak ties." You connect with them only on occasion, perhaps once a month or even only two or three times a year. But once you've made the connection, you can keep it alive with an occasional email, phone call, cup of coffee, or hallway chat at a conference you both attend. And once you've made the links, each outpost will know your interests and can let you know if anything of consequence to your world occurs in theirs.

Like all networks, a strategic network works only if it's built on mutual interest. You serve as an outpost in your world for those who serve you in theirs. You learn their interests and goals and let them know if anything in your world might concern them.

Leadership and management are largely based on the future, on a sense of where you and your group are trying to go, the future you want to create. To define, move toward, and succeed in that future, you need to proactively build a far-flung network of people who live and work at the edge of your current world.

Linda A. Hill is the Wallace Brett Donham Professor of Business Administration at Harvard Business School. **Kent Lineback** spent many years as a manager and an executive in business and government. They are the coauthors of *Being the Boss: The 3 Imperatives for Becoming a Great Leader* (Harvard Business Review Press, 2011).

Develop a Big-Picture Perspective

CHAPTER 7

Spotting Trends and Patterns That Affect Your Business

by Nina A. Bowman

As organizations strive to be more agile, and competitive forces demand a greater ability to anticipate and adapt, individuals need to understand not only what objectives they're striving toward but also what key trends may affect these goals. Managers at all levels will need to "lift up" and find a greater balance between current-day demands and big-picture needs. As Rosabeth Moss Kanter demonstrates in chapter 11, the best leaders know when to focus in and when to pull back.

Lifting up requires you to keep an eye out for the weak signals of change that may impact your role, department, or business. These signals can come from within your company or the external environment.

Observe Signals Inside Your Organization

[handwritten annotations: → Find creatl value ; Intern Department]

Start by paying attention to the internal signals within your company that may give rise to opportunities or challenges right under your nose. In many organizations, the heavy demands of day-to-day work and short-term goals lead to a myopic view of the business that can lead to flawed decision making and negative outcomes. Consider a marketing manager who misses the signs of his company's broader financial struggles and presents an unrealistic budget. Or an HR manager who works tirelessly to hire highly sought-after tech talent but ignores the signals of falling retention rates in the existing employee base.

To identify the relevant changes happening within your company, look for trends related to different aspects of your function. Notice signals related to people, process, products, and strategy. The types of questions shown in table 7-1 can help you uncover the weak signals of internal change.

After you reflect on these questions, draw connections between the data by considering possible implications of these changes. Ask yourself, *What might these changes mean for me and my department?* and *How will these signs in my department impact stakeholders in other*

TABLE 7-1

Questions to help you identify signals of internal change

People	Process
• Have there been any new hires or departures of key employees in the company? Has there been an increase in external hires? • Have there been important changes in relationships and power dynamics that could impact your efforts? • What is your sense of employee engagement, and how might that impact the speed and quality of your initiatives?	• What key process or technology changes are occurring in other departments? • Are there patterns in the types of requests you are receiving from key stakeholders? What might these requests signal? • Has your team experienced a change in the service they receive from internal colleagues?

Products	Strategy
• How might the introduction of a new product, service, and geography by your company impact your line of business? Does a series of new products signal a change in direction? • Are there signals that a drop in sales of a key product might be due to internal factors?	• Does a series of acquisitions signal a new direction for the organization? • Are there changes in resource allocation across the company? • Are there signals that stakeholder priorities have changed?

parts of the business? By asking these questions, you'll realize where your own strategy and priorities may need to adapt.

Additionally, consider the root cause of these changes by asking "why?": *Why is employee engagement dropping on my team?* or *Why are there increased requests from selected areas of the business?* Understanding root cause can help you find a solution to the problem you're facing or a better path forward if change requires it.

Study Trends Outside Your Company

In exploring root causes, you will also need to consider external forces affecting your business. External monitoring has long been the purview of dedicated internal strategy teams, external consultants, or forward-looking executives. But for organizations to be able to respond more quickly to outside patterns and trends, all managers must see this as an important task worthy of their time. Failure to pay attention to external signals—or waiting until a signal becomes strong before acting—can have harsh consequences.

At times of broad and fast change, you need to actively observe changes in your market and encourage your employees to collect and share relevant external information as well. First, specify what information is important to gather and how often you need to look for it. Your department's function and the degree of change in your industry will determine how much effort to place on external monitoring. Routine monitoring efforts may suffice for more stable industries, while more dynamic industries, such as tech, may require more frequent action.

It's important to draw from a broad array of sources. Doing so will likely unearth a trend faster than relying on one stream of information alone. Consider these different sources of information as you conduct your search:

- **News and competitor updates.** Regularly browse headlines across publications, explore conversation patterns in social media, and track competitors' new product offerings and press releases. Ask yourself, *Which information is most relevant to the work I do?* Consider, for example, someone who develops toys for a living. He should take note of headlines that indicate shifts in buying habits or social media complaints about product features. If a competitor is developing a new tech-savvy toy for childhood learning, he would also want to jot that down to discuss with his team.

- **The latest research.** Reach out to your industry and trade associations or local chambers of commerce for the latest trend reports, and dig into key data sets from relevant federal bureaus. What patterns may have a direct impact on your business? For someone in the toy industry, these reports may reveal industrywide trends in toy sales as well as changes in who customers are and where they are making their purchases.

- **People in your network.** Conversations with former coworkers or friends who work at competitor companies can help you find out what others are seeing and how they're reacting. For example, the toy developer may attend conventions and toy fairs, and set up coffee meetings with members of his network there. He can then ask, *What trend is most interesting to you right now? Why do you think that's happening? Any concerns about the industry? What are you excited about?*

- **Macro trends.** Demographic, economic, social and cultural, technological, and political trends, like those discussed in chapter 10, can have direct and indirect effects on your industry and your organization. For example, for toy companies, technological trends would come into play as younger children spend more time on tablets and smartphones. Average income data for key sales regions would also be important to consider when making pricing decisions.

- **Sources outside your core area of business.**
  Familiarity with our own industry and business can often blind us to what's new or evolving. By looking at an industry you're less familiar with, you can spot inconsistencies and commonalities. Look to other industries or fields and ask, *Could this happen in my company, or my department?* The toy developer may look into outdoor recreation, book publishing, the entertainment industry, or other activities that children and families do together when they're not playing with toys.

As you and your team gather information, encourage your employees to share early observations and concerns. Plan small group discussions on market signals or schedule meetings to identify what you're missing that enable weak signals to come to light.

Examining weak signals requires teams to become comfortable with exploring what might initially seem like a "silly idea." Your team may be hesitant to do so at first. Support your team members by making it safe to discuss these fledgling ideas. Then decide which signals are worth continuing to monitor, focusing on trends with impact—those with a broad scope and the ability to endure over time. To sort out the important information from the noise, ask, *Could this trend have significant impact on market share or sales?* Or *Does this trend have the potential to exacerbate the company's weaknesses?*

Move from Information to Insights

To find value in your research, you must connect these seemingly random external and internal signals and translate them into usable insights. By combining internal information with external observations, you can find new ways to overcome challenges or new opportunities to pursue.

Let's say that you're a manager at a skin-care manufacturer and you notice a drop in sales of moisturizing lotion. On a first review of internal sales data, you may simply conclude that the company's branding efforts are ineffective, or that you need to tweak product placement or price. But when you consider external trends as well, you discover other potential causes for the dip. A trend that "consumers are increasingly pressed for time" may indicate that users are dropping the task of putting on moisturizer altogether. Warmer temperatures may mean customers are swapping out the lotion in favor of sunscreen. These findings can lead you to different proposed solutions—perhaps considering partnerships with other products, so that a busy individual can combine using the moisturizer with already established routines, or identifying other products you might sell during warmer seasons to make up for the drop in sales. These options could be much more effective than simply changing placement, price, or branding.

The following tips can help you convert seemingly disparate trends and observations into strategic insights:

- **Detect patterns by looking at information and data over time.** Patterns may not be obvious in the short term but often become clearer as we look at data over time, such as six months, one year, three years, or more. But don't wait too long to react. Analyzing employee engagement numbers, for example, can reveal a lot about your employees' job satisfaction and what they value, so you can continue this activity over time to find ways to improve the workplace. But if you begin to see signs of increased negativity and decreased productivity, you'll want to respond to the situation quickly, before critical team members leave the company.

- **Categorize the information into common themes.** Information gathering can quickly become overwhelming. Organizing your findings into common themes can decrease the number of items the brain needs to process, allowing you to see connections more easily. If you notice trends that involve customer shopping patterns—even across differing industries—group them together and see if there are connections to your company's offerings.

- **Discuss the implications of trends.** Not every trend you identify will matter. As a bank manager, you may not need to spend too much time analyzing a general trend that individuals are moving closer to cities. But if this data shows that more people are renting homes, rather than buying them—particularly in the region where you operate—this may indicate a decrease in loan requests in the future. By focusing on implications, you can find the trends that have the potential to impact your space.

- **Explore peripheral ripple effects.** It can be easy to ignore trends that don't have a direct impact on your environment, but it is important to explore the longer-term consequences or ripple effects before declaring a trend "unimportant." For example, the increasing number of people using social media was seemingly unrelated to the service industries—that is, until users started posting reviews and complaints on social platforms.

- **Combine trends and build multiple scenarios for the future.** Meaningful insights often arise when we combine different trends and then ask the question, "What would happen if . . . ?" If you're in a medical profession, for example, you may notice changes in health-care offerings by insurers, increasing concern by individuals about how they'll afford treatment, and more families hesitant to vaccinate children. By combining these trends, you can ask yourself, "What would happen if kids suffer from rare diseases and can't afford medication? What options can I offer my patients in these situations, and what will this mean for other patients in the community?" By thinking through three or four plausible scenarios for how selected trends might unfold, you can decrease your response time if a particular scenario arises.

⊙ **Ask the big questions.** Insights are a product of the questions asked. Ask bigger questions and you will get bigger insights. A manager in the leadership and development space may ask, "How can I prepare John to be a more effective leader?" and get a short-term response. Instead, they should ask, "How will age demographics affect our overall leadership pipeline?" This broader question will lead to a set of actions that can position the company for the long term.

In lifting up to see trends and patterns, it's important to realize that your biggest roadblock may not be the information itself but managing your own analysis. Our assumptions and unconscious biases may cloud our objectivity, which can cause us to see a trend that we want to see, rather than what is actually there.

Take conscious steps to prevent these tendencies. Openly challenge your assumptions, look for data that goes against your beliefs, and craft discussions with your team that allow individuals to let go of current constraints so you can decrease the effects of bias and create the conditions for effective strategic discussions. With greater awareness, you can observe trends more accurately and lift up in a manner that supports the organization objectively.

Nina A. Bowman is a Managing Partner at Paravis Partners, an executive coaching and leadership development firm. Previously, she held various advisory and
leadership roles in strategy. She is an executive coach
and speaker on issues of strategic leadership, leadership
presence, and interpersonal effectiveness. She is also a
contributing author to the *HBR Guide to Coaching Employees* (Harvard Business Review Press, 2015).

CHAPTER 8

Look at Your Company from the Outside In

by Graham Kenny

I was once appointed CEO of a company in need of a turnaround. We made trusses and frames for houses. One morning, after I'd been on the job about three months, I found myself staring out my window, watching the trucks and forklifts below, and I thought: *What am I doing here? Can I, on the fingers of one hand, list the ingredients of success in this industry?*

Adapted from "Customers Are Better Strategists Than Managers" on hbr.org, September 23, 2014 (product #H010B8); and "Five Questions to Identify Key Stakeholders" on hbr.org, March 6, 2014 (product #H00PH9).

In the weeks and months that followed, the senior management team and I made a number of major decisions about the company's future. As a team, I observed, we were busy doing things and making changes, all of which made sense to us as managers. But as time progressed, I returned to these questions, over and over: *How well do we know what our customers want? How well do we know what our suppliers and employees expect? What would it take to meet those needs better than our competitors could?*

In short, I'd begun to think in a way that I'd now call "strategic." Up until that point, most of my focus had been on saving the company from ruin, which had led largely to "operational" thinking—worrying about the proper staffing numbers, the ratio of overhead costs to direct costs, the prices we were paying for supplies, how machinery was utilized in the plant, the overstocking and obsolescence of products used in manufacturing, the cash flow for the business, that sort of thing.

It was after I left that job and started working as a consultant that the penny finally dropped: I realized I'd been looking at the business from the inside out. From that perspective, all I could see was the activity that consumed my day. I also realized that customers and other stakeholders have the opposite perspective. Their view is outside-in—and that's what makes them good strategists.

Think about it: As a customer, how often do you ask yourself, "Why don't they . . . ?" When you go to a department store, do you note which products should be added or removed? If you could have your way with the store's presentation, would you change the layout, the lighting, and perhaps the color scheme? How about the service? No shortage of suggestions there, right? So it goes with airlines, telephone companies, banks, every organization you deal with: You're continually redesigning strategic factors such as product range, presentation, and customer service. We all do it.

Now try doing that for own your organization. Suddenly it's much harder, because it requires an outside-in view. Here are my suggestions for making it easier.

Tap Your Stakeholders

If your company's two-day offsite involves a group of senior executives getting together to develop a strategic plan, and they do so right there and then, my guess is it's not a *strategic* plan at all. It's an operational plan. Your management team is most likely looking inside-out, and it surely doesn't have all the answers. It probably hasn't even asked the right questions.

Effective leaders *listen*. They *observe*. And they *translate* what they learn into strategy. Hubris has no place in outside-in thinking and effective strategy development. You have customers and other stakeholders who are dying to share their ideas about how you should change your company in ways that will make them even greater supporters. So empower them to do that. (The box "Five Questions to Identify Key Stakeholders" will help you create a focused list.)

FIVE QUESTIONS TO IDENTIFY KEY STAKEHOLDERS

Suppose you're meeting to determine who your key stakeholders are. People will submit their ideas, and in no time at all you'll have a large list—and potentially a nightmare. If you don't focus on the relationships that matter most, management and staff will be running in all directions, not meeting anyone's needs very well.

To produce a shorter, more coherent list, answer the following questions about each contender you've identified in your brainstorming session.

1. Does the stakeholder have a fundamental impact on your organization's performance? *(Required response: Yes.)*

   Example: A manufacturer of trusses and frames for houses decided, on reflection, that a local council wasn't a key stakeholder. Though the council set regulations that the company had to follow, those rules didn't have much of an effect on sales or profits the way, for instance, customers did.

2. Can you clearly identify what you want from the stakeholder? *(Required response: Yes.)*

   Example: Members of a law firm's strategic planning team knew they wanted revenue from clients, productivity and innovation from employees, and continued funding from partners—yet they couldn't specify what they wanted from the community. That relationship wasn't deemed key.

3. Is the relationship dynamic—that is, do you want it to grow? *(Required response: Yes.)*

   Example: A company that ran 17 retirement villages had a dynamic, strategic relationship with current and potential residents. It wanted increased occupancy and more fees for services used. The company's relationship with a university, by contrast, was static and operationally focused. It involved only a fixed amount of research funding and co-branding each year. Though the co-branding generated broader awareness and may have indirectly yielded more residents and revenue, the university itself didn't achieve key stakeholder status.

4. Can you exist without or easily replace the stakeholder? *(Required response: No.)*

   Example: A professional services firm in HR that had taken out a loan initially listed the bank as a stakeholder. But ultimately, that relationship didn't qualify as key, because the loan could be easily refinanced through another source.

5. Has the stakeholder already been identified through another relationship? *(Required response: No.)*

(continued)

FIVE QUESTIONS TO IDENTIFY KEY STAKEHOLDERS

Example: A government department involved in planning and infrastructure listed both employees and unions as key stakeholders. But this amounted to double counting: The unions represented employees' interests, and the organization's primary relationship was with its employees.

After you've applied the above criteria, your list will certainly be shorter, but it may still feel a bit unwieldy. If that's the case, try to combine categories. By clustering stakeholders according to common needs, you'll whittle your list down to a more manageable length, increasing the efficiency and impact of your efforts to meet the right groups' needs.

Conduct interviews to understand your stakeholders' needs. You want to hear, for example, how customers decided to buy from you or from the competition. You want to find out how employees committed to join your organization or decided to leave to work somewhere else, how suppliers agreed to enter into contracts to provide you with goods or services when they had a choice, and how partners signed up to sponsor your events when there were plenty of other options to consider. You're looking for insight into their "journey" with the organization, to put this in marketing terms. On the criteria that emerge from their stories, you want to know how your organization performs—and what suggestions people have for improving your competitiveness.

Each interview should take place soon after the customer's shopping trip, the supplier's experience with your company, and so on. Wait too long, and people will forget important details and convey only vague impressions.

Go Beyond Your Current Customers

Interview potential stakeholders, too. That includes customers and others who are currently dealing with your competitors—but also those who interact with neither you nor your rivals. In the wine industry, you would talk to people who don't drink wine—beer and cocktail consumers, for example—in order to appreciate why they prefer these other beverages, understand fully any objections they might have to wine, develop ways to eliminate any barriers to purchase, and figure out how to appeal to them in order to disrupt their pattern of choice. This is how you glean insights into new areas of competitive advantage.

Listening to your stakeholders—both current and potential—will give you a new perspective on your organization and what you're offering. By looking at your organization from the outside in, you can adjust your company's positions on the factors that matter.

————————

Graham Kenny is the Managing Director of Strategic Factors, a Sydney, Australia–based consultancy that specializes in strategic planning and performance measurement, and the president of Reinvent Australia. He is the author of *Crack Strategy's Code: Build and Sustain Your Competitive Edge* and *Strategic Performance Measurement: Boost Your Organization's Performance—By Measuring It.*

CHAPTER 9

Thinking Long-Term in a Short-Term Economy

by Ron Ashkenas

Do you find it odd that when a company announces a profit of $8.4 billion in a single quarter, the performance is reported as "disappointing"? Or $5.7 billion as "dreadful"? Fact is, these were the terms used by analysts to describe the results produced by Exxon Mobil and Royal Dutch Shell after their second-quarter earnings release in 2012.[1]

Adapted from "Thinking Long-Term in a Short-Term Economy" on hbr.org, August 7, 2012 (product #H0097Q).

Almost all publicly traded firms are given "qualitative assessments" by analysts during earning announcement season, which influence investors. But too often the weight of Wall Street opinion causes executives to focus on hitting short-term earnings targets rather than creating long-term value. And even if executives' strategies are not playing to short-term expectations, they still have to spend a lot of time explaining why this quarter's earnings are not up to snuff.

So despite Exxon Mobil's and Shell's robust, multi-billion-dollar profits, analysts deemed the results "disappointing" and "dreadful" compared with previous quarters. And they use these terms even while acknowledging that the industry is facing lower oil prices, increased availability of natural gas, decreasing economic activity, and rising costs—all factors largely outside of the companies' immediate control. The analysts also say that in the face of all this, both companies continued to make long-term investments and still delivered billions of dollars in profit. How is that "disappointing"?

Unlike Exxon Mobil and Shell, many other companies end up making decisions—such as laying off staff or overpaying for an acquisition—to appease these quarterly earnings pressures. In fact, one of the surest ways to increase stock prices in the short term is to announce a significant layoff.

However, the reality is that most organizations can't be judged on a quarter-to-quarter basis. Strategies take time to unfold and bear fruit, and managers need time to develop their own capabilities and those of their teams. Yes, it's important to achieve short-term results as a way to test new approaches and build confidence, but these need to be put into the context of long-term value creation. Otherwise we run the risk of sacrificing our future.

But how do you keep the focus on long-term value creation while the media and the markets exert pressure to do the opposite? Here are a few thoughts, not just for CEOs, but for all managers:

First, make sure that you have a dynamic, constantly refreshed strategic "vision" for what your organization (or unit) will look like and achieve three to five years from now. I'm not talking about a strategic plan, but rather a compelling picture of market/product, financial, operational, and organizational shifts over the next few years. Develop this with your direct reports (and other stakeholders) and put the key points on one page. This then serves as a true north to help guide key decisions.

Second, make sure that your various projects and initiatives have a direct line of sight to your strategic vision. Challenge every potential investment of time and effort by asking whether it will help you get closer to your vision, or whether it will be a building block to help you get there. Doing this will force you to continually rebalance your portfolio of projects, weeding out those that probably won't move you in the right direction.

Finally, be prepared to take some flak. There may be weeks, months, or quarters where the results are not on the rise, or don't match your (or analyst) expectations. Long-term value, however, is not created in straight lines. As long as you're moving iteratively toward the strategic vision on a reasonable time line, you're probably doing the right things. And sure, you can always do more. But just make sure that you're doing things for the right reasons.

Ron Ashkenas is an Emeritus Partner with Schaffer Consulting, a frequent contributor to *Harvard Business Review,* and the author or coauthor of four books on organizational transformation. He has worked with hundreds of managers over the years to help them translate strategy into action. He is the coauthor of *Harvard Business Review Leader's Handbook* (Harvard Business Review Press, 2018).

NOTE

1. Clifford Krauss and Stanley Reed, "For Exxon Mobil and Shell, Earnings Fall with Energy Prices," *New York Times*, July 26, 2012, http://www.nytimes.com/2012/07/27/business/global/royal-dutch -shell-earnings-tumble-13-in-first-quarter.html?_r=3.

CHAPTER 10

The Future Is Scary. Creative Thinking Can Help

by Alan Iny and Luc de Brabandere

Having a long-term view can be a struggle. In an effort to plan for a future we can't clearly see, we search for ways to reduce uncertainty and risk. But doing so can thwart fresh thinking that opens our eyes to new possibilities. Instead, we learn to embrace uncertainty—and create more opportunity for our team and organization—by thinking creatively.

Thinking creatively about the future requires sensitivity to the complex, fast-moving world in front of you, the

Adapted from "The Future Is Scary. Creative Thinking Can Help" on hbr.org, September 18, 2013 (product #H00DZG).

ability to anticipate unexpected disruptions, and a willingness to constantly reevaluate your most basic beliefs and assumptions. Done well, we believe thinking about the future of your organization in this way requires doing three things.

Understand How People Think

The way the brain is hardwired could be leading you and your colleagues to hold on to tired assumptions and misperceptions about your organization. People have a natural bias toward ideas and concepts that confirm, rather than contradict, those they already believe. Such biases can sabotage their capacity for fresh thinking.

A classic example: Henry Ford famously insisted that the all-black Model T would always remain desirable to consumers. Even as other automakers created new car models and colors, and his colleagues urged him to consider pursuing new directions, Ford refused to budge. After years of fantastic innovations that helped bring the automobile to the masses, Ford fell prey to the *anchoring bias* that leads people to make (or fail to make) new decisions by referencing their previous experiences.

Free your mind to generate new ideas by noticing how these and other cognitive patterns may be shaping your key assumptions and holding you back from thinking in more creative ways. When thinking about the future of your organization, ask yourself whether "the way we do things here" is necessarily still relevant—and encourage your colleagues to do the same. Insist on a culture that allows people to constantly challenge the hypotheses and assumptions they have about your organization, the industry in which it does business, and the world in which it operates.

Question Your Organization's Fundamental Beliefs

To think creatively is to change the way you look at something—to update one or more of your mental models. To get started, drill down on some of the most important mental models that you and your colleagues are currently using by conducting a "beliefs audit." Interview or survey your colleagues to understand their thoughts about your organization's current situation. Consider the following questions:

- What are some key assumptions inherent in your day-to-day activities—established "rules" under which you or your organization generally operate? What core values are "given"?

- What are some of your own beliefs about your organization, and what makes it perform effectively at present? In what areas does your organization devote too much—or too little—time and resources?

- What is your organization's competitive space, and are there ways it might be redefined?

- If you or your organization didn't exist, what difference would it make to the world? What would be missing?

These are only sample questions—you should develop others based on the current needs of your organization.

Questioning your current situation can open up paths to creative thinking. For instance, Google's original aspiration was to build the best search engine ever; arguably the organization achieved that. But in order to enter a new era of growth, Google leaders needed to perceive their company differently. Only when they challenged their long-held assumption that "We are a search engine company" could they then come up with the "We want to know everything" concept that sparked projects such as Google Earth, Google Book Search, and Google Labs, along with further improvements to their fabled search engine.

Use "Prospective Thinking" to Consider Key Trends and Disruptions

Take an expansive, long-term view. Be open to all possibilities and fully aware of what's happening both within and outside of your organization or your immediate environment.

Trends, a topic that was covered in more detail in chapter 7, can have a great impact on your business and provide new opportunities for competitive advantage. *Megatrends*—large social, economic, political, environmental, or technological changes likely to have major impact across a wide range of areas—can be a very useful tool to help spark new possibilities. Examples include the rise of alternative energy sources, rapidly developing markets like Brazil and China, and increasing mobile connectivity. Megatrends will affect your company, your customers, and your competition as well as your family and community.

Develop a list of issues you believe will likely play out over a relatively long period of time (say, 5 to 10 years, though different industries could have longer or shorter time frames), have a strong and wide-reaching impact, and open up a range of strategic responses on your part. Then refine your list by asking: "Which trends will be the key vectors for shaping my organization's future?" "What are some of the seemingly irrelevant trends that could end up being surprisingly critical?"

Ponder the many ways you could exploit these megatrends to create new opportunities for your organization. Stretch your thinking by considering which of these trends your organization would be the *least* ready to deal with. Are there trends right in front of you that you haven't yet addressed?

Ask yourself how these potential trends could influence the new ideas you want to generate for the future. For example, a client we worked with several years ago, a major European department store chain, stated emphatically that its future was in China, based on trends outlining the increased purchasing power of the rising middle class there. But not a single person on the leadership team had heard of Taobao, the closest Chinese analogy to Amazon.com, which was growing at double-digit rates, building new distribution centers across the country, and focusing on customer relationships and loyalty.

Thinking creatively about the future is not only about gathering the trend data but maintaining the atmosphere of doubt cultivated in the first step. This will enable you to look at data—whether trends, customer research, or competitive intelligence—in fresh ways, to be better prepared for an uncertain future. Indeed, thinking creatively about the future means embracing the uncertainty, rather than trying to remove it.

Alan Iny is senior global specialist in business creativity at The Boston Consulting Group (BCG). Luc de Brabandere is a senior adviser with the firm. They are coauthors of *Thinking in New Boxes: A New Paradigm for Business Creativity.*

CHAPTER 11

Zoom In, Zoom Out

by Rosabeth Moss Kanter

After an explosion on a BP oil platform in the Gulf of Mexico in April 2010 killed 11 people and caused the biggest oil spill in U.S. history, the company's CEO at the time, Tony Hayward, zoomed in on the implications for his career. He appeared preoccupied with the incident's impact on BP's management and, particularly, on himself. About a week after the explosion, Hayward was quoted as saying to executives in his London office, "What the hell did we do to deserve this?" Despite PR coaching, a month later he told reporters, "I'd like my life back."

Hayward, who was forced to resign in July, had numerous opportunities to acknowledge the bigger picture:

Reprinted from "Managing Yourself: Zoom In, Zoom Out" in *Harvard Business Review*, March 2011 (product #R1103K).

the human devastation and public consternation in the Gulf region. But even though BP deployed thousands of engineers to contain the spill, he could not, in public, rise above a 10-foot view; it was as though the crisis were his own personal devil. Hayward repeatedly focused on the small picture—trying, for example, to shift the blame to supplier Transocean, which had run the rig that exploded. His zoom button seemed to be stuck on the closest setting.

The lens through which leaders view the world can help or hinder their ability to make good strategic decisions, especially during crises. Zoom in, and get a close look at select details—perhaps too close to make sense of them. Zoom out, and see the big picture—but perhaps miss some subtleties and nuances.

Zoom buttons on digital devices let us examine images from many viewpoints. They also provide an apt metaphor for modes of strategic thinking. Some people prefer to see things up close, others from afar. Both perspectives—worm's-eye and bird's-eye—have virtues and pathologies. But they should be vantage points, not fixed positions. Leaders need multiple perspectives to get a complete picture. Effective leaders zoom in and zoom out.

I've come to this conclusion after more than 25 years of observing how leaders set strategic direction, interact with constituencies, and respond to unexpected events. I've worked with thousands of executives and conducted systematic studies of innovation, alliances, change, and transformation in hundreds of organizations. I've seen how organizational structures, processes, and cultures can direct the gaze of leaders close in or far out, and how levels of analysis can become default positions that limit effectiveness.

The zoom framework offers a dynamic model that can help current and aspiring leaders increase their own range of vision and establish conditions that enable others' success. In this article, I will identify the behavior and decision modes associated with zooming in and contrast them with those for zooming out. I'll consider the structures and cultures that trap people in dysfunctional default positions, and I'll conclude with ideas on developing capabilities for zooming to all levels.

Zooming In

Zooming in brings the details into sharp focus. Any opportunities look large and compelling, though they may lack some context.

A CEO I will call "John Jones"—who owns a midsize retail chain started by his father—works primarily in close-in mode. A classic entrepreneur who combines hustle with retail-is-detail know-how, Jones expanded the chain successfully from two to 30 locations by continually seeking the next prime site, merchandise item, or website tip. His discoveries came mostly through his personal connections rather than analysis. Jones disdained strategic plans and management theories. He removed a well-regarded banker from his advisory board, for instance, because the banker would ask for plans—orderly goals, with timelines—when Jones simply wanted to concentrate on specific operational ideas that were easy to implement.

Thanks to his industry knowledge, wide personal network, and intuition, zooming in served Jones well for a decade. But when the economy soured, his good instincts felt insufficient. Family members and key employees began to question his decisions. Jones had no succession plan—nobody had been groomed for the future. He made acquisitions on the basis of his own taste or just because an owner wanted to sell and gave little thought to cost, whether the acquisition was a good fit, or what else was on the horizon. He had no broad theory about which opportunities to pursue and no industry map. Zooming in was limiting his company's growth prospects.

Close-in managers look for immediate benefits and make ad hoc decisions. They often favor one-on-one conversations over group meetings. They want to address details by doing whatever occurs to them. Faced with a problem, they look for quick fixes rather than stand back to seek underlying causes, alternatives, or long-term solutions. They prefer to contact someone they know rather than search more widely for expertise. These tendencies are exacerbated in organizations that restrict information flow, reward quick hits, and confine people to their roles.

A close-in perspective is often found in relationship-intensive settings, where human talent is the primary asset. Consider another executive, whom I'll call "Sam Lee." He ran a well-regarded professional services firm during a decade of incremental growth. Known as a benign leader, Lee could talk about strategies with external constituents, but he operated best when zooming in. He liked to confer in a clublike huddle in his office rather than discuss issues in open meetings. He was unfailingly helpful with individual requests (including one-off favors). In other words, he liked to make exceptions instead of policies. As a result, his organization had an abundance of private deals with individual staff members (such as off-calendar budget allocations, vacation privileges, sabbaticals, and extended family leaves).

In a time of prosperity with few external threats, a personal approach may be acceptable. Toward the end of Lee's tenure, however, the firm found itself in an increasingly competitive environment with greater regulatory pressure. It was becoming untenable to treat each situation as unique. Even as policy exceptions accumulated, the logic behind these decisions remained unaddressed. Junior professionals were left to wonder and worry about the rules and fairness. Whispered concerns about favoritism ran through the corridors. The organization was running on a patronage system of personal credits and debits, with a market for favors substituting for principle-based decision making. Morale and productivity declined, jeopardizing the company's reputation and making it harder to attract the best talent. When Lee retired, his successor immediately zoomed out, stating a few broad strategic priorities. He created clear formal policies to replace informal exceptions and began discussing them all openly in large meetings.

One of the traps of zooming in is that policies and systems are based on internal politics. Close-in people tend to talk about their personal lives, as though self-disclosure will beget the same from others, turning organizational actions into an exchange of favors based on special relationships. They often resist change because it disrupts the social equilibrium. Sometimes their personal approach is valuable, because people respond faster to individuals they know than to abstract appeals. But "Do it for me" is a weak basis for corporate decisions. It also means that employees cannot easily stand in for one another, because relationships are "owned" by specific people. And it can put ego above institution.

Relying heavily on personal instinct and interpersonal deals without a wider perspective or a long-term rationale can prove perilous. An overly personal approach can also make managers quick to perceive slights, whether or not they're real. The CEO of one technology company, though known as a great strategist, still let zooming in drive some decisions. He was personally offended by how a prominent magazine had portrayed him, so the company stopped advertising there. Employees took this as a warning to tread carefully when providing him with unfavorable information. In another case, a corporate middle manager pored over emails to see whether he was being treated appropriately, and complained immediately if he perceived any suggestion of offense. His focus on status over substance cost him a higher-paying position; the plum promotion went instead to a manager with a grasp of the bigger picture.

Zooming in can obscure the big picture, leading managers to overlook important issues. Decisions become based on who you are and whom you know, not on broader goals.

Zooming in can also lead to turf protection. When managers use territorial language, it reveals that they have fallen into this trap. One division CFO, for instance, always used the first person when referring to budget numbers, as in "I have x dollars," even though it was the organization's money, and ignored repeated requests from other members of the executive group to stop this manner of speaking.

Personalizing is not the same thing as self-reflection—indeed, it might be the opposite. Self-reflection is a learning process that requires a distant perspective on one's own behavior, in context. An obsession with self is reinforced by zooming in, but self-awareness stems from zooming out.

Zooming Out

Zooming out is essential to big-picture decision making. When people are far out, they can map the whole territory before taking action. They see events as examples of general patterns rather than as idiosyncratic or personal incidents. They put things in context and stress principles.

The former CEO of Garanti Bank, Akin Ongor, led it from a middle-of-the-road bank in Turkey to global prominence by setting up processes that replaced poor performers and upgraded talent. When his announcement of layoffs provoked union protests and even death threats, Ongor refused to take the attacks personally or get drawn into ad hominem battles. Instead, he went to the media and elevated the discussion to the principles behind the bank's actions. By zooming out, he helped his employees, the public, and government officials see the layoffs in the context of a transition in the economy and as a move that would save an important institution so that it could create more jobs in the future. The protests ended, and Ongor continued to lead successful change at the bank.

Zooming out helps people see the map and stay focused on larger principles. Consider Procter & Gamble CEO Robert McDonald, who rose through the ranks to head a global public company with a long-established culture. Even while seeking current profits, he constantly asks questions about what will support the sustainability of the company and keep its values intact. He can generalize about geographies and lines of business while appreciating cultural differences. He is personable but doesn't personalize issues, repeating often that he is a steward of an institution that must endure beyond him.

Zooming out is appropriate for top leaders. But it also has traps. For one thing, key stakeholders might want to see immediate results and know that the details are right before they support long-term big-picture thinking. That's why broad visions need to be matched by small wins that demonstrate feasibility. For another, leaders who like to be far out may operate so high above the fray that they don't see emerging threats and opportunities (which, ironically, is a danger for close-in leaders too) or recognize competing theories that are better able to explain new developments. Having zoomed out to examine all possible routes, they can neglect to notice the moment for action on one promising path. When zooming out makes established highways look too good, leaders may fail to jump onto a side road to get around the traffic.

When the focus is on grand theory, novel situations are dismissed as too insignificant to merit attention. Leaders lose the sense that the big picture might be contingent on a set of circumstances that may well evolve. But sometimes a novelty is a signal, heralding embryonic change. The film *The Social Network* presents a fictionalized version of an iconic moment in which the Winklevoss brothers, feeling aggrieved that fellow student Mark Zuckerberg had created Facebook when he was supposedly working on their web venture, meet with the university president, a disguised version of then–Harvard president Lawrence Summers. In the movie, the president dismisses Facebook as just another undergraduate venture and tells the brothers to forget it and start another business rather than waste his time on something so trivial. Whether the incident was merely movie fiction or not, in real life that president was overly focused on important long-term plans and goals and on keeping a wide perspective on the institution. His lack of attention to interpersonal interactions eventually cost him support and his job.

Sometimes leaders need a nudge to look at details that might shake their theories. Take a chief executive I'll call "Herman Fry," who ran a science-based company that was starting to use genetic engineering in a growing product line. Fry had previously led a division to global prominence through breakthrough innovations and was known as a brilliant strategist and big-picture thinker. But when he heard rumblings against genetically modified ingredients in Europe, he initially dismissed them as local issues that didn't require scrutiny or a response. When he heard that a U.K. customer was being pressured about the same issue, his attention was caught—but not enough; he still said the concern was a minor blip and did not bother to look more deeply. By the time he was persuaded to gather more details, a global backlash had begun, and the company had lost the chance to reassure customers and tell its story ahead of the protests.

A preference for zooming out can make leaders appear remote and aloof. After a campaign that involved both inspiring rhetoric and street-level organizing, President Barack Obama faced severe national crises. He zoomed out to address big systemic issues, such as the financial crisis, with policies that advisers said stopped further erosion. But critics said that he failed to convince average Americans that he was addressing their problems. His supporters argued that his actions, Keynesian in nature, would show their merits in the longer run; yet as John Maynard Keynes himself pointed out, in the long run we're all dead. One of the problems with staying at the most distant end of the zoom is that the picture looks static and few routes are visible. It may appear, for instance, as though all economic highways go through the Federal Reserve and big banks. Zooming in and monitoring the situation as it appeared to communities and families, might have helped Obama communicate that he was seeking alternatives that would reach more people directly—such as increasing small-business lending at local banks. Instead, despite his many accomplishments, Obama's approval ratings plummeted, and his party lost badly in the 2010 elections.

Getting Stuck

A failure to zoom can spell doom. As we have seen, problems arise when people get stuck at one end of the scale and are unable to move to the other for a different perspective.

One question is whether it's possible to create teams that balance close-in and far-out modes. Perhaps. But if people can't shift from the worm's-eye or bird's-eye level, they often talk past one another. Those zooming in want to come back to the particulars and haggle over details, frustrating those who want patterns and a strategy. Those zooming out might seem theoretical and impractical, or find that their general frameworks and principles are not understood by those who zoom in. Hardened preferences can get in the way of good decisions.

A narrow focus in either direction can lead to trained *incapacity*, a concept attributed to social theorist Thorstein Veblen. Regardless of their innate potential, if people spend too much time on tasks that draw on only part of their repertoire, it can make the other part atrophy. The fact that it's difficult to balance zooming in and zooming out may explain one perceived difference between male and female managers uncovered by INSEAD professor Herminia Ibarra. She found that women score high on all aspects of "21st century" leadership performance (such as relationship building, collaboration, and teamwork) except vision setting. Relationships are nurtured by zooming in. Vision involves zooming out. This may derive from the pernicious stereotypical view that men should be entrusted with big-picture decisions, while women should be assigned to caretaking tasks. The very nature of caretaking requires zooming in to be attentive to details, one child or one executive at a time. Zooming in is also a necessity for those whose fate depends on being attuned to the characteristics and preferences of power holders. Traditional divisions of labor by gender encourage men to zoom out and women to zoom in, with fewer opportunities to take another perspective.

Zooming Toward Both Perspectives

The best leaders work the zoom button in both directions. Faced with a crisis, they can address the immediate situation while seeking structural solutions. They can zoom in to see problems while zooming out to look for similar situations, root causes, and principles or policies that will help prevent the crisis from recurring.

Daniel Vasella, chairman and former CEO of pharmaceutical giant Novartis, was both a psychiatrist by training—which made him able to zoom in on the emotional state of the people around him—and a strategist with a theory of industry change that guided divestitures, acquisitions, and internal restructuring. He stressed personal values as well as global trends. Indra Nooyi, PepsiCo's CEO, blends a big-picture view of principles guiding the company, such as the need for transformation in food and beverage companies to promote improved health, with an ability to zoom in on the details of budget allocations for current business lines. Nooyi has defined new roles (such as a chief science officer) and new structures (for instance, the Global Nutrition Group, linked to central R&D) that help the previously decentralized organization both zoom out to a global perspective and zoom in on local differences.

Effective leaders encourage others to expand their zooming range. For example, P&G, like most companies in the consumer packaged goods industry, is a heavy user of large-sample survey market research, which maps territories through statistical abstractions, a form of zooming out. Though P&G's leaders don't disregard these data, they also send employees into the field to live with families, zooming in on their needs and experiences. The closely observed details of individual household behaviors ultimately influence P&G's investment decisions.

The zoom function is more than a metaphor; it can be a way for people to stretch their mental capabilities by, for example, manipulating maps, comparing photos, exploring issues from various vantage points, and creating action plans that reflect learning from multiple perspectives. IBM's Corporate Service Corps integrates both the big and the small pictures into its global leadership development programs. It sends culturally diverse teams on monthlong field assignments in unfamiliar territory. The team members get direct experience solving specific problems on the ground while gaining a broad view across countries and cultures.

The language of zooming offers an objective way to discuss differences in perspective and encourage people to move to a different level: "Let's zoom in on that problem." "Let's zoom out to put it in perspective." Zoom-based checklists can help people stop themselves from overpersonalizing, reminding them to go up a few levels

TABLE 11-1

Are you stuck in a perspective that's too close in?

Telltale signs	Questions that will help you zoom out
• You get overwhelmed by countless details.	• What is the context? What matters most?
• You take things personally, finding the "me" angle first.	• What larger purpose is being served? What is at stake for others?
• You trade favors, hoping others will "do it for me."	• Why is the task or mission worthy of support?
• You make exceptions or special deals based on particular circumstances.	• Will the circumstances recur? What policies or decision frameworks could be used?
• You jump on any good-looking offer that pops up.	• Does this fit the goal or destination? What else might be on the horizon?
• You treat every situation as unique.	• Are there other similar situations? What categories or groupings make sense?

to the principles involved, or from overgeneralizing, encouraging them to get more grounded in situational realities. Everyone can apply the principles of zooming to his or her own job by asking the right questions, such as whether a given action fits the overall goal or whether there is sufficient information to move forward on a particular theory. (See table 11-1, "Are you stuck in a perspective that's too close in?" and table 11-2, "Are you stuck in a perspective that's too far out?")

The zooming idea suggests that we don't have to divide the world into extremes—idiosyncratic or structural, sit-

TABLE 11-2

Are you stuck in a perspective that's too far out?

Telltale signs	Questions that will help you zoom in
• You dismiss deviations from plans or models as too minor to matter.	• Does the deviation challenge the model? How can the deviation be understood?
• You veer away from dealing with specific problems in favor of focusing on general theory.	• What actions does your theory suggest for this particular problem?
• You must have a full analysis or a big study before determining actions.	• Is there sufficient information to proceed in this instance? What are the costs of delay?
• You always stay on major established paths.	• Are there side roads or shortcuts?
• You pursue the mission regardless of human costs.	• How is this affecting the people who must carry out the mission?
• You fit everything into a few general categories.	• What are the details that make things different? Which details matter?

uational or strategic, emotional or contextual. The point is not to choose one over the other but to learn to move across a continuum of perspectives. President Bill Clinton's political genius was that he could "feel your pain" while putting events into historical and international context, zooming in and out quickly in a single conversation or speech. That dynamic capability is the essence of great strategic thinking.

Zooming can help leaders respond to events before they become crises. It can help them embrace new opportunities while continuing to operate with principles that build sustainable institutions for the long run. Leaders should make room to zoom.

Rosabeth Moss Kanter is a professor at Harvard Business School and Chair and Director of the Harvard Advanced Leadership Initiative. Her latest book is *MOVE: Putting America's Infrastructure Back in the Lead*. Follow her on Facebook and Twitter @RosabethKanter.

Align Decisions with Strategic Objectives

CHAPTER 12

Reflect on Your Actions and Choices

by Liane Davey

Being more strategic doesn't mean making choices that affect the whole organization or allocating scarce budget dollars. It requires only that you put even the smallest decisions in the context of the organization's broader goals. Nurturing a relationship that could provide unique insight into a supplier, a customer, or a competitor is highly strategic. Everyone has an opportunity to think more strategically.

If you're not being seen as enough of a strategic thinker, my guess is that it's because you're so busy.

Adapted from "Strengthen Your Strategic Thinking Muscles" on hbr.org, January 21, 2014 (product #H00MVH).

Between meetings, emails, phone calls, and other immediate demands, there's often not much time left for work that requires deep thought. The result is decisions that are based more on *reflex* than on *reflection*. The risk of these reflexive, knee-jerk decisions is that they tend to be based on what has worked before. That would be fine if our world were static, but it is not. Your industry, your competitors, and your customers are changing at an unprecedented rate. Doing what you've always done can be as risky (or more risky) as trying a new and unproven approach.

In this context, it's critically important to make time to reflect before making decisions: *What is involved? Who is involved? What is at stake? What is the opportunity and what are the risks?* What at first seems like an opportunity might reveal significant risk, and what seemed risky at first might reveal a significant opportunity.

Your other response to your harried life might be to make a list of things to accomplish, put your head down, and get things done. But focusing too narrowly restricts your chance to be strategic. Strategic people create connections between ideas, plans, and people that others fail to see. Consider this example: A senior banking executive was looking for a new IT vendor for operations in the Caribbean when he learned that another department was working on new customer service standards. His default reaction was to just carry on. But that would have been a lost opportunity to marry the system requirements with the new service standards, which would create better protocols for customer interactions with more efficient and effective data available in real time.

And remember, relationships are strategic too. The executive asked the new IT vendor to introduce him to other clients who had already implemented their new systems. This gave him the chance to ask questions about the vendor and how to optimize the contract and the relationship.

Strategic people see the world as a web of interconnected ideas and people, and they find opportunities to advance their interests at those connection points.

But a person who *reflects* on situations and *connects* ideas and people still has one problem: It isn't possible to do everything! Possibilities are unlimited; time, money, and resources are not. That necessitates the ability and willingness to make choices—to decide what you will do and what you won't. Closing one door in favor of another requires the courage to take action (for which you could later be blamed) and confidence to abandon an alternative (which could be a missed opportunity). It is at the point of choice that your ability to be strategic is finally tested. Making a choice isn't without risks, but the risk of not choosing—of spreading limited resources over too many options—is greater. You will be seen as more strategic if you take action and course-correct than if you choose to stagnate and do nothing or stall because you're trying to do everything.

You don't need a new title, more control, or bigger budgets to be more strategic; you just need to be more deliberate in your thoughts and actions. By investing time and energy to reflect on the situations and decisions that face you; by finding ways to connect ideas and people that you had never linked before; and by having the courage to make choices about what you will do and what you won't, you will greatly increase your strategic contribution.

———————

Liane Davey is the cofounder of 3COze Inc. She is the author of *You First: Inspire Your Team to Grow Up, Get Along, and Get Stuff Done* and a coauthor of *Leadership Solutions: The Pathway to Bridge the Leadership Gap*. Follow her on Twitter @LianeDavey.

CHAPTER 13

Seven Steps for Making Faster, Better Decisions

by Erik Larson

Managers make about three billion decisions each year, and almost all of them can be made better. The stakes for doing so are real: Decisions are the most powerful tool managers have for getting things done. While a tool like goal setting is aspirational, making decisions actually drives action. People usually do what they decide to do.

The good news is that there are ways to consistently make better decisions by using practices and technologies based on behavioral economics. In a three-month

---

Adapted from "A Checklist for Making Faster, Better Decisions" on hbr .org, March 7, 2016 (product #H02PR2).

study of 100 managers, my team and I found that managers who made decisions using best practices achieved their expected results 90% of the time—and 40% of them exceeded expectations.

But although there's great potential for using best practices to improve decision making, many organizations are not doing it. In a study of 500 managers and executives, we found that only 2% regularly apply best practices when making decisions, and few companies have systems in place to measure and improve decision making over time.

There are three reasons why this gap between potential and practice exists:

- **History.** Decision making in business has long been more art than science. That is partly because, until recently, most managers had relatively little access to accurate information. Few decision tools are widely used; the pros-and-cons list, popularized by Benjamin Franklin, is probably the most common—and it's nearly 250 years old. And then there is the unfortunate circumstance that economics in the 20th century was based on the theory that people make rational choices when given good information, a theory proved to be somewhere between spotty and completely wrong, thanks to a revolution in behavioral economics, led by Nobel Prize winner Daniel Kahneman.

- **Psychology.** We are predictably irrational. Behavioral economists have uncovered a range of mental shortcuts and cognitive biases that distort our perceptions and hide better choices from us. Most business decisions are collaborative, which means groupthink and consensus work to compound our individual biases. Further, most business decisions are made under the stress of high uncertainty, so we often rely on gut feelings and intuition to reduce our mental discomfort.

- **Technology.** Enterprise software has automated many managerial tasks over the past 40 years. That shift has formed a foundation for better decision making, but it leaves the job unfinished. Behavioral economics shows that providing more complex and ambiguous information does little to help managers and their teams with the main challenges they must overcome to make better decisions.

So what can be done?

Through our work and experiments with thousands of decision makers, my team and I found that the most successful decision-making approach boils down to a simple checklist. But simply understanding the items in the list is not enough. This checklist must be *used* to be effective, since our biases don't go away just because we know they are there.

Each time you face a decision, use these steps as a tool to counteract your biases:

1. **Write down five preexisting company goals or priorities that will be impacted by the decision.** Focusing on what is important will help you

avoid the rationalization trap of making up reasons for your choices after the fact.

2. **Write down at least three, but ideally four or more, realistic alternatives.** It might take a little effort and creativity, but no other practice improves decision making more than expanding your choices.

3. **Write down the most important information you are missing.** We risk ignoring what we don't know because we are distracted by what we *do* know, especially in today's information-rich businesses.

4. **Write down the impact your decision will have one year in the future.** Telling a brief story of the expected outcome of your choice will help you identify similar scenarios that can provide useful perspective.

5. **Involve a team of at least two but no more than six stakeholders.** Getting more perspectives reduces your bias and increases buy-in—but bigger groups have diminishing returns. According to research by Marcia Blenko, Michael Mankins, and Paul Rogers of Bain & Company, once you've reached seven people in your group, each additional member reduces decision effectiveness by 10%.[1]

6. **Write down what was decided, as well as why and how much the team supports the decision.**

Writing these things down increases commitment and establishes a basis to measure the results of the decision.

7. **Schedule a decision follow-up in one to two months.** We often forget to check in when decisions are going poorly, missing the opportunity to make corrections and learn from what's happened.

Our research has found that managers who regularly follow these seven steps save an average of 10 hours of discussion, decide 10 days faster, and improve the outcomes of their decisions by 20%.

We need a new, scalable approach to managing decision performance. It must replace the historical theory of rational choice. It must acknowledge that our psychology often leads us astray. And it must use simple, friendly tools like this one, designed to have an outsize impact on how managers and teams make decisions.

––––––––––

Erik Larson is founder and CEO of Cloverpop, a cloud solution that applies behavioral economics and collaboration to help businesspeople make better decisions together. He is a graduate of MIT and Harvard Business School, a decorated U.S. Air Force officer, and an experienced technology executive based in San Francisco.

NOTE

1. Marcia W. Blenko, Michael C. Mankins, and Paul Rogers, *Decide and Deliver* (Boston: Harvard Business Review Press, 2010).

CHAPTER 14

How to Make Better Decisions with Less Data

by Tanya Menon and Leigh Thompson

Maria, an executive in financial services, stared at another calendar invite in Outlook that would surely kill three hours of her day. Whenever a tough problem presented itself, her boss's knee-jerk response was, "Collect more data!" Maria appreciated her boss's focus on the data, but as the surveys, reports, and stats began to pile up, it was clear that the team was stuck in analysis paralysis. And despite the many meetings, task forces, brainstorming sessions, and workshops created to solve

Adapted from "How to Make Better Decisions with Less Data" on hbr.org, November 7, 2016 (product #H038UJ).

any given issue, the team tended to offer the same solutions—often ones that were recycled from previous problems.

As part of our research for our book, *Stop Spending, Start Managing*, we asked 83 executives how much they estimated that their companies wasted on relentless analytics on a daily basis. They reported a whopping $7,731 per day—$2,822,117 per year! Yet despite all of the data available, people often struggle to convert it into effective solutions to problems. Instead, they fall prey to what Stanford University professor James G. March and his coauthors describe as "garbage can" decision making: a process whereby actors, problems, and possible solutions swirl about in a metaphorical garbage can and people end up agreeing on whatever solution rises to the top.[1] The problem isn't *lack* of data inside the garbage can; the vast amount of data means managers struggle to prioritize what's important. As a result, they end up applying arbitrary data to new problems, reaching a subpar solution.

To curb garbage-can decision making, managers have to think more strategically about which information they need to solve a problem and how it should be applied in their decision making and actions. We recommend the "data DIET" approach, which provides four steps of intentional thought to help convert data into knowledge and wisdom.

Step 1: Define

When teams and individuals think about a problem, they likely jump right into suggesting possible solutions.

Indeed, many brainstorming sessions begin this way. But while the prospect of "problem solving" sounds positive, people tend to fixate on familiar approaches rather than stepping back to understand the contours of the problem.

Instead, start with a *problem-finding mindset*, where you loosen the definitions around the problem and allow people to see it from different angles, thereby exposing hidden assumptions and revealing new questions before the hunt for data begins.[2] With your team, think of critical questions about the problem in order to fully understand its complexity: How do you understand the problem? What are its causes? What assumptions does your team have? Alternatively, write about the problem (without proposing solutions) from different perspectives—the customer, the supplier, and the competitor, for example—to see the situation in new ways.

Once you have a better view of the problem, you can move forward with a disciplined data search. Avoid decision-making delays by holding data requests accountable to if-then statements. Ask yourself a simple question: *If I collect the data, then how would my decision change?* If the data won't change your decision, you don't need to track down the additional information.

Step 2: Integrate

Once you've defined the problem and the data you need, you must use that information effectively. In the example above, Maria felt frustrated because as the team collected more and more pieces of the jigsaw puzzle, they weren't investing the same amount of time to see how the pieces fit together. Their subconscious beliefs or assumptions about problems guided their behavior, causing them to follow the same tired routine time and time again: collect data, hold meetings, create strategy moving forward. But this is garbage-can decision making. To keep the pieces from coming together in an arbitrary fashion, you need to look at the data differently.

In design thinking, you break down the problem and then synthesize it, putting the pieces together again. One technique you can use with your team to integrate the different elements of the problem is the KJ diagram (named after its creator, Kawakita Jiro). The goal is to sort discrete facts and data points into causal relationships. Write the facts on notecards and then sort them into piles based on observable relationships—for example, an increase in clients after a successful initiative, a drop in sales caused by a delayed project, or any other data points that may indicate correlated items or causal relationships. In doing this, you can create a visual model of the patterns that emerge and make connections in the data.

Step 3: Explore

At this point in the process, you may have some initial ideas or solutions based on your KJ diagrams. Now's the time to develop them. To facilitate collaborative exploration, one of our favorite exercises is what we call the "passing game": Assign distinct ideas to each team member and give each individual five minutes to develop it by drawing or writing in silence. Then have them pass their work to a teammate, who continues drafting the idea while they take over a teammate's creation.

Discuss the collaborative output. Teammates recognize how it feels to give up "ownership" of an idea and how it feels to both edit and be edited; they also recognize their implicit assumptions about collaboration. The new perspective forces them to confront directions that they didn't choose or never would have considered. You can also add multiple sequential passes (like a telephone game) to demonstrate the idea's unpredictable evolution as three or four teammates play with it. After allowing people this space for exploration, discuss the directions that are most fruitful.

Step 4: Test

The last dimension requires team members to use their powers of critical thinking to consider feasibility and correct for overreach. Design tests to see if your plan for moving forward will work. Under which types of situations will the solution fail? Select a few critical tests and run them. While people often over-collect data that supports their prior beliefs—a tendency known as confirmation bias—people under-collect disconfirming data. By running even a single test that fights this bias, you can see what you need to see, even if you don't want to.

Instead of ignoring the data entirely or getting over-loaded by it, think strategically about your data needs. This involves doing more with less—widening, deepening, integrating, extending, and testing the data you do have to convert it into knowledge and wisdom. In practicing the mental exercises we've described with your team, you can curb your appetite for data while getting better at using the data you have.

———

Tanya Menon is an Associate Professor of Management and Human Resources at the Ohio State University's Fisher College of Business. **Leigh Thompson** is the J. Jay Gerber Professor of Dispute Resolution and Organizations at the Kellogg School of Management and the author of *Creative Conspiracy: The New Rules of Breakthrough Collaboration* (Harvard Business Review Press, 2013). They are the coauthors of *Stop Spending, Start Managing: Strategies to Transform Wasteful Habits* (Harvard Business Review Press, 2016).

NOTES

1. Michael D. Cohen, James G. March, and Johan P. Olsen, "A Garbage Can Model of Organizational Choice," *Administrative Science Quarterly* 17, no. 1 (March 1972): 1–25.

2. J. W. Getzels, "Problem-Finding and the Inventiveness of Solutions," *Journal of Creative Behavior* 9, no. 1 (March 1975): 12–18.

Set Priorities and Manage Trade-Offs

CHAPTER 15

A Better Way to Set Strategic Priorities

by Derek Lidow

Smart leaders understand that their job requires them to identify trade-offs, choosing what *not* to do as much as what *to* do. Grading the importance of various initiatives in an environment of finite resources is a primary test of leadership.

To meet this challenge, leaders often turn to rank ordering their priorities; it is natural and easy to make a list. When I work with leaders on the crucial task of priority setting, however, I caution against rank ordering.

Adapted from "A Better Way to Set Strategic Priorities" on hbr.org, February 13, 2017 (product #H03FAI).

It can be tremendously demotivating to managers to be assigned a rank, and it all but guarantees dissension and turf wars between team members.

A better way to establish priorities is to put rank ordering aside and return to first principles. There are three interdependent variables that are essential for executing any initiative: objectives, resources, and timing. You can't produce a project's desired effect without precise objectives, ample resources, and a reasonable time frame. If you push or pull on one leg of this triangle, you must adjust the others.

All three variables are important, but resources reign supreme. Resources are what enable an objective to be accomplished within a set time; without dedicated means, an initiative is pure fantasy. Once a leader decides what resources will be allocated to achieve which objectives over what periods of time, there is no more need for ranking. The leader will be forced to acknowledge three kinds of priorities: critical, important, and desirable.

Three Types of Strategic Priorities

A *critical* priority is an objective that must be successfully accomplished within a specified amount of time, no matter what. For example, it might be critical that a company win a new order (which will be awarded on a given date) from a major customer, or get a factory fully operational by a certain day. If the objective of winning the order is set and the timing is nonnegotiable, then the only element you can manipulate is resources (money, people, equipment). If the leader is sincere about the priority, then they must make all the resources requested available to the project manager. Though leaders may not realize it, declaring a project "critical" implies that it must be accompanied by a de facto blank check, enabling the manager to draw on all other available resources within the organization. And all critical priorities are, by definition, equal within the category.

An *important* priority, on the other hand, is an effort that can have a significant positive impact on performance. For these initiatives, resources are fixed and the variable is either time or the objective. For example, an organization may have an aspirational goal but fix the resources that it feels it can afford to invest over a specified time. A leader might say, "Let's assign Miguel and Aisha to this project full time for the next quarter." The organization, if it is operating rationally, should be willing to accept however much improvement it can get from that fixed investment. Alternatively, an organization may declare that it will invest a specified amount of resources for as long as it takes to achieve an objective: "We're going to assign Miguel and Aisha to install the new software, however long that will take." An important priority implies that the organization be understanding when the objective is variable and patient when time may vary.

A *desirable* priority is an effort in which resources and time are both variables. The organization desires an outcome but cannot absolutely commit specific resources over any specifiable time period: "Whenever Miguel and Aisha are not required on our critical product launch, they will work on installing the software upgrade." Progress will be made only when and if resources become available.

Because resources are fixed for all critical and important priorities, the potential "blank check" resources that may be required to hit a critical project must all come from desirable tasks. You cannot in good conscience set a critical priority unless you also designate desirable projects from which resources will be immediately transferred to the critical objective when required.

Allocate Resources and Plan Priorities

Once you have identified critical, important, and desirable projects, you can begin to identify appropriate objectives, resources, and time for each one. Use the following four-step process, which is also illustrated in figure 15-1.

Step 1. List in one column the resources (people, money, highly constrained elements like a sample bus for demonstrating products) available for all proposed projects. For example, you might have 10 salespeople on the East Coast, 7 on the West Coast, 4 in the Midwest, and 3 in the South; a travel budget of $10,000; and one sample bus.

Step 2. List across the top row the projects, improvements, or initiatives you want to accomplish with those resources with any existing time constraints. For example, you might write, "Renew clients in all four regions; win a contract with IBM by the time your new plant opens on March 1; get Salesforce.com in all regions but on a staggered schedule."

Step 3. Indicate in the appropriate cell how the available resources would be allocated in a scenario where everything proceeds as expected. For example, three salespeople in each region might be devoted to renewing customer contracts, while seven salespeople, the sample bus, and half of the travel budget might go toward winning the IBM contract.

Step 4. Declare which one or two projects are critical, designating which additional resources from the matrix can be called on by the critical objectives when and if needed. (If you declare more than one project critical, you must keep in mind that they cannot potentially depend upon the same pool of on-call resources.) For example, if the IBM contract is critical, you would ask the project head—in this case, your lead IBM salesperson—what additional resources might conceivably be needed if the going gets tough, and where those resources might come from. That could include some of the IT resources from the Salesforce implementation on the East Coast, which means that the Salesforce effort is now categorized as desirable and that you cannot expect your people to fulfill the objective by a certain time. Projects that are not critical but aren't on call to potentially provide resources to a critical project now fall into the important category, where time or the objective is flexible.

As the projects and resources are listed and the group figures out how best to allocate resources and

FIGURE 15-1

Example spreadsheet for strategic priorities

Step 1: List resources

East Coast sales (10 people)						
West Coast sales (7 people)						
Midwest sales (4 people)						
Southern U.S. sales (3 people)						
Travel ($10,000)						
Sample bus						
IT resources (6 people)						

Step 2: Add projects, improvements, or initiatives

	Renew all clients	Win IBM contract by March 1	East Install Salesforce by March 1	West Install Salesforce by ?	Midwest Install Salesforce by ?	South Install Salesforce by ?
East Coast sales (10 people)						
West Coast sales (7 people)						
Midwest sales (4 people)						
Southern U.S. sales (3 people)						
Travel ($10,000)						
Sample bus						
IT resources (6 people)						

Step 3: Allocate resources

	Renew all clients	Win IBM contract by March 1	East Install Salesforce by March 1	West Install Salesforce by ?	Midwest Install Salesforce by ?	South Install Salesforce by ?
East Coast sales (10 people)	3 people	7 people				
West Coast sales (7 people)	3 people	4 people				
Midwest sales (4 people)	3 people	1 person				
Southern U.S. sales (3 people)	3 people					
Travel ($10,000)	$5,000	$5,000				
Sample bus		X				
IT resources (6 people)			6 people			

Step 4: Decide on one or two critical projects

	Renew all clients	Win IBM contract by March 1	East Install Salesforce by March 1	West Install Salesforce by ?	Midwest Install Salesforce by ?	South Install Salesforce by ?
East Coast sales (10 people)	3 people	7 people				
West Coast sales (7 people)	3 people	4 people				
Midwest sales (4 people)	3 people	1 person				
Southern U.S. sales (3 people)	3 people					
Travel ($10,000)	$5,000	$5,000				
Sample bus		X				
IT resources (6 people)			6 people			

time constraints among the potential initiatives, this matrix becomes a strategy document. As projects are completed, leaders can revisit the process to reallocate resources that have been freed up. They can also reallocate resources if a crisis occurs—which by definition creates a critical priority. The same is true with a change of strategy.

The transparent allocation of resources and the specifying of responses to changed conditions align the team and head off dissension. Managers no longer feel that giving up resources reduces their status. They are playing an essential role in executing a critical priority. And they are content to be governed by the fair, inexorable logic of realistic priority setting instead of rank ordering that doesn't add up.

Derek Lidow teaches entrepreneurship, innovation, and creativity at Princeton. He was the founder and former CEO of iSuppli Corporation and is the author of *Startup Leadership*. His newest book is *Building on Bedrock*. Follow him on Twitter @DerekLidow.

CHAPTER 16

How to Prioritize When Your Manager Is Hands-Off

by Amy Jen Su

Prioritizing work can be frustrating, especially if you work for a hands-off manager or a company that doesn't give you clear goals. Most of us face this reality daily. The frequently cited research of Robert Kaplan and David Norton shows that more than 90% of employees don't fully understand their company's strategy or know what's expected of them to help achieve company goals.[1]

Adapted from "How to Prioritize Your Work When Your Manager Doesn't" on hbr.org, January 24, 2017 (product #H03EVL).

Compounding the problem, research from Strategy& shows that global executives say they have too many conflicting priorities.[2]

In a world where clashing and unclear objectives are the norm, how can you learn to prioritize your own work and still feel satisfaction from a job well done?

Take Ownership

First, check your mindset when it comes to setting priorities. Don't assume that prioritizing your workload is someone else's job, and don't choose to see yourself solely as a "do-er" or a "worker bee." It's easy to point blame at our managers and organizations when we experience high levels of stress or an overwhelming amount of work. Recognize that consciously setting priorities is a key pillar of success.

Filter Priorities

Select a couple of areas to set priorities in; this can help the brain manage information overload. Many researchers have found that it's the overload of options that paralyze us or lead to decisions that go against our best interests. Two criteria I use with clients to filter for priorities include *contribution* and *passion*. Consider your role today and answer the following questions:

- **What is my highest contribution?** When we reflect on contribution, we consider both the organization's needs and how we uniquely bring to bear strengths, experience, and capabilities. The word *contribution* captures a sense of purpose, citizenship, and service.

- **What am I passionate about?** Motivation and
energy fuel action, so when setting priorities, get
clear on what brings you inspiration in your work
today.

Determine Next Steps with an Organizing Framework

We can put the two criteria of contribution and passion
together to create an organizing framework. This framework can help you to sort priorities and define subse-
quent actions. Look at the matrix in figure 16-1.

Quadrant I: Prioritize those areas of your job that hit this
sweet-spot intersection of bringing your highest value-
add and making an impact that you feel excited about.
Consider how you answered the two questions about
your contribution and your passions. Which projects,
initiatives, and activities show up on both lists?

Quadrant II: Tolerate those parts of the role that are important but drain your energy when you're engaging in
them. What are the possible discomforts, and what can
you do about them?

- Tolerate and accept that you aren't going to love
every part of the job. For example, you may be
excited about having a larger role and team but
less excited about the increase in managerial processes and administration that come with it.

- Tolerate the fact that you may be on a learning curve. Perhaps a key part of the job includes

FIGURE 16-1

Which tasks should you prioritize?

Focus on those that align your passion with where you can contribute most. Tolerate, elevate, and delegate the rest.

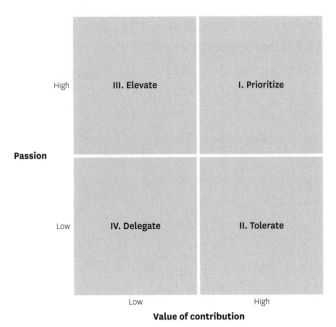

Source: Paravis Partners

something that isn't yet a strength, such as presenting at town hall meetings or being more visible externally. Keep a growth mindset and push yourself out of the comfort zone.

- Remember that there is a tipping point in this quadrant. For example, your highest contribution in a strategy role may never offer you the passion you feel when coaching people. The quadrant could highlight that it's time for a change (which was my situation more than 15 years ago, when no amount of prioritizing was ever going to overcome the fact I was in the wrong career).

Quadrant III: Elevate those tasks that give you a lot of energy but that others don't see as the best use of your time. Where are the possible points of elevation?

- Elevate the value-add. Perhaps you see a hot new area, but the impact is less clear to others. Share what you are seeing out on the horizon that fuels your conviction, and explain why it's good not only for you but also for the company.

- Elevate yourself. Be mindful of areas that you still enjoy, perhaps from a previous role or from when the company was smaller. Maybe you love to fix problems and have a bias toward action, which leads you to get involved in things your team should be handling. Hit "Pause" before diving in.

- Ultimately, if the disconnect grows between what keeps you motivated and what your organization values, it may be time to move on.

Quadrant IV: Delegate the daily churn of low-value and low-energy-producing activities, emails, and meetings. If there's no one to delegate to, make the case for hiring someone. You may also be able to just say no, or eliminate those tasks altogether. The irony is, as we progress in our careers, things that were once in quadrant I now belong in quadrant IV. If people still come to you for these tasks, graciously redirect them by saying something like, "It's so great to see you. I know how important this is. I've asked Kate on my team to take on those issues, and she'll be able to get you a more direct and speedy answer."

Operationalize and Flag Priorities in Your Calendar

Look back on your calendar over the last month to see how much time you allocated across the four quadrants. (I highlight each one in a different color in my calendar to quickly see how I'm doing: QI = yellow, QII = purple, QIII = blue, QIV = no color). At the start of a week, flag all QI priorities and give yourself a little extra preparation time on them.

Don't settle for the status quo. As Greg McKeown, the author of *Essentialism,* observes, if you don't prioritize your time, someone else will.[3] And it won't always be with your best interests or the greater good in mind. Take ownership and reclaim decision-making power over where you can best spend your time and energy. By doing so, you set yourself on a trajectory to produce meaningful results, experience more job satisfaction, and have increased energy.

––––––––––

Amy Jen Su is a cofounder and Managing Partner of Paravis Partners, a boutique executive coaching and leadership development firm. She is coauthor, with

Muriel Maignan Wilkins, of *Own the Room: Discover Your Signature Voice to Master Your Leadership Presence* (Harvard Business Review Press, 2013). She holds an MBA from Harvard Business School and a degree in psychology from Stanford University. Follow Amy on Twitter @amyjensu.

NOTES

1. Robert S. Kaplan and David P. Norton, "The Office of Strategy Management," *Harvard Business Review*, October 2005 (product #R0510D).

2. Paul Leinwand and Cesare Mainardi, "Stop Chasing Too Many Priorities," hbr.org, April 14, 2011.

3. Greg McKeown, "Prioritize Your Life Before Your Manager Does It for You," hbr.org, June 1, 2015 (product #H02422).

CHAPTER 17

Identify and Kill Outdated Objectives

by Jessica Avery

When we think of strategic action, we often focus on what new things we should start doing: What projects should our department or team take on to contribute to the organization's end goal? What innovative business ideas should we pursue? While this forward thinking is essential, many managers forget a key step in achieving those results: leaving the past behind.

In his book *The Three-Box Solution*, Tuck School of Business professor Vijay Govindarajan introduces three "boxes" for allocating an organization's time, energy, and resources:

Box 1: Manage the present by optimizing core businesses.

Box 2: Forget the past by letting go of the values and practices that have lost relevance.

Box 3: Create the future by inventing a new business model.

As managers strive to run a high-performing business, Boxes 1 and 3 tend to get most of the attention, while Box 2 is often forgotten. Deciding whether to leave something behind—especially if it's a project you've devoted a lot of time and attention to—can be a tough choice. But just as it's important to identify what you should be contributing, it's essential to recognize and stop doing tasks and projects that interfere with or distract from valuable work.

Human Nature and the Aversion to Letting Go

As humans, we're emotional beings, and our emotional attachment to initiatives can often stand in the way of a clear analysis of how much value they bring. The time and effort we've invested in a project in the past often blinds us to what it may contribute in the future. We need to put those emotions aside to judge the initiative on its merits and learn to let go.

In an ideal world, we'd be able use pure logic to make these strategic choices on what to cut. Think of *Star Trek*'s Mr. Spock when he assesses situations on the USS

Enterprise. Unencumbered by emotion, his decisions on how to proceed come down to three simple steps:

1. He estimates the value of what he's currently doing.

2. He estimates the value of what else he could do.

3. He then compares the two values. As soon as he sees that the alternative creates more value than the current option, he switches to that new path.

Spock is constantly evaluating options and making adjustments accordingly. The trade-offs that must be made for each decision come down to the basic idea of opportunity cost. *Opportunity cost* is the value of what you aren't doing but could be doing. It's the value of the new store that you aren't opening, the new product you aren't launching, or the additional sales you'd get from a new marketing approach that you aren't executing on.

In general, we undervalue opportunity cost because it feels fuzzier and is harder to quantify than "real costs." But being hard to value doesn't mean that it has no value—opportunity cost may be the biggest cost that your company has. Think of how much the opportunity cost would have been if Apple had chosen to pass on the iPhone and concentrated instead on its core computer business. Simply put: If the value of what you are doing now is lower than the value of what you could be doing instead, you need to change course—and in business, that may mean letting go of work that had been successful in the past.

Say you want to add a new product line in your company. You calculate the potential value of the product line at $100,000 per year. But there's a snag—in order to launch the new line, you'd have to take three sales and marketing employees off supporting a current product, which generates $50,000 a year and has been a solid seller for the company. However, this product's sales are starting to decline. In this case, it makes sense to let go of the solid seller (lose up to $50,000) in favor of the bigger, more profitable opportunity (gain $100,000).

Assessing opportunity cost for new objectives is a guessing game, and so it will always feel risky, especially when your emotions get in the way. But *not* taking advantage of an opportunity can hold even bigger risks. Your team's attachment to a "classic" product—one you've dedicated years to creating and selling—could mean wasting a lot of time and money on something that may no longer have value. These old projects ultimately become "zombie projects." They live on because they've always been there, creating less and less value over time but refusing to die. Think about the social media team that spends hours writing dedicated social promotions that show no significant increase in sales. Or the marketing manager who creates email newsletters that have low open and click rates. Every minute that people spend working on an out-of-date objective is one where they are missing out on significant amounts of money by not contributing to the priorities that matter. (To see an example, see the box "The Curious Case of Telex.")

THE CURIOUS CASE OF TELEX

Telex machines started as a bold new replacement for business-to-business telegrams in the 1930s, reaching their heyday in the early 1980s. After that, the growth of fax machines and then email made them increasingly cumbersome and expensive by comparison—and ultimately obsolete.

Yet it wasn't until 2008 that AT&T and British Telecom finally closed down their Telex operations. For two decades, they continued to serve the shrinking market of companies that found it hard to let go of their Telex machines, even as they could use them to communicate with fewer and fewer people. In retrospect, having a Telex machine in the 1990s or 2000s, using up support fees and employee time and expertise, seems crazy.

But how does the Telex machine get killed?

The company's Telex expert who is checking the machine hourly for urgent messages and maintaining it with paper, ink, and repairs may realize that the number of messages is decreasing. But does he want to suggest switching to checking messages once a day? Or switching to faxes or email? By doing that, he risks being perceived as a complainer who just wants to do less work. Worse yet, he could lose his job if people agree the Telex is unnecessary and don't think he can contribute in other ways. His coworkers don't want to insult him by pointing out that his job is obsolete, and

(continued)

THE CURIOUS CASE OF TELEX

certainly, there are a few clients who might still use the Telex, so what's the harm in keeping it around?

The "harm" is that spending time and energy on this outdated device means that other, more pressing needs aren't getting the attention they deserve. If the company shifts away from Telex early, one-off clients may be briefly inconvenienced as they learn to communicate via other means, but internal teams would free up time to devote to other, more important goals—like bringing in additional clients and generating more revenue for the organization.

Part of the reason switching to new opportunities is so hard is because of the *status quo bias*. Humans have evolved to have a strong preference for keeping things the same; we're averse to change. This trait can be very useful, for instance, when it kept early humans from leaving the cave at night while the saber-toothed tigers were roaming. But it also means we remain wedded to projects and processes in our work simply due to habit. And it leads to inertia in organizations.

With emotions running high and a human inclination toward status quo bias, the deck is stacked against Box 2 efforts. It therefore requires a *lot* of active energy to break out of this inertia.

Assess What to Cut—and Finally Let Go

So if it's difficult to clearly define opportunity cost and human nature encourages us to remain the same, how do you decide what to stop pursuing and implement that change? Start by asking the right questions of the initiative or task.

Make a project prove its worth

When looking at a potentially outdated project or objective, we tend to wait until we get unanimous consensus that there's no harm in abandoning it. This default approach is wrong on three levels:

- **Consensus generally arrives too late.** By the time the process is so thoroughly obsolete that *everyone* agrees that it should be stopped, you've probably wasted years of resources that you should have redeployed.

- **It puts the burden of proof in the wrong place.** We require proof that stopping a project will cause no harm, but instead, we should be asking ourselves, "Can we prove that the project is creating value now?" Flipping the burden of proof in this way becomes a powerful lever for change.

- **It looks at the value of the project in a silo.** Deciding whether there's no harm in abandoning an old process or initiative project takes the value it creates as a stand-alone benefit, rather than comparing it to the value of what you would do instead. Doing something that adds $1,000 may seem worth doing—but if you are so busy with your current business you can't put resources into new endeavors that may add $10,000 of value if properly resourced, you are saving dimes but losing dollars.

To agree to continue pursuing something, you have to make the case for keeping it, taking into account other options and alternatives. For example, for a company using an outdated method of communication like Telex machines, this means asking, "What is the additional value created by receiving messages on the Telex rather than streamlining all communication to modern systems? What would we do with the extra money and employee time if we stopped supporting the Telex network?"

If the existing part of the business can prove that it's adding more value than what you would do instead, then the organization should keep it. But if can't, that's a signal that it should be discarded.

Create a process for winnowing large, medium, and small projects

Projects come in a variety of sizes. Organizational resources are devoted to some large, strategic goals, but they're also used for thousands of little tasks that you and your team tackle on a daily basis. Figure 17-1 illustrates the many projects that make up the work in your company—from large, organizational objectives that affect

FIGURE 17-1

Organizational work comes in many sizes

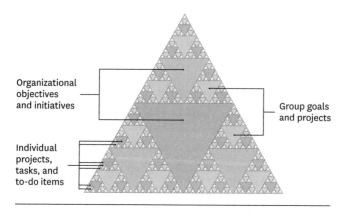

Organizational objectives and initiatives

Group goals and projects

Individual projects, tasks, and to-do items

the entire workforce (the largest triangles) to group projects and goals that affect your unit (the mid-size triangles) to small daily tasks on an individual's to-do list (the hundreds of smallest triangles). Each of these three areas benefits from a different approach when deciding what—and how—to cut.

Large goals above your group. Unsurprisingly, the biggest triangles use the largest amounts of resources, and cutting such objectives would allow significant resources to be deployed to more valuable alternatives. Deciding whether one of these triangles should be removed requires answering two key questions: What is the value that they are creating? And what is the value of what else we would be doing?

As a manager, you may not have the ability to answer these questions or make these large-scale cuts in your organization. Changing projects or processes that affect companywide strategic objectives instead requires a top-down approach. These cuts will likely be highly visible and, unless these activities or products have become obsolete and are creating zero value, getting rid of them will be thorny and contentious. Arguments between groups of stakeholders will likely stall the process until upper management steps in to make the hard decision.

Midsize goals within your group. As a manager, you can act as identifier, evaluator, and often decider on the many midsize projects and to-do items that are primarily in the domain of your group. Keep your group's core goals in mind at all times and ask yourself whether what you and your team are doing is necessary for a given goal: Why are we doing the task? Does it add value? Has that value been shrinking? For instance, is your group creating reports that don't generate follow-up questions? Are you managing customers who buy less and less? Are you marketing to segments that are becoming less relevant?

Look for clues that may indicate an incipient zombie task: less feedback from stakeholders and less urgency around the task. For instance, if there's a delay, are there repercussions? Listen to your gut: If doing a task gives you a vague feeling of pointlessness, you may be working on an emerging zombie item.

Small tasks within your group. A large portion of the work of a group is the hundreds of smaller tasks that keep everyone busy. Individually, these tasks don't have much impact if they become zombies—they may add a few minutes back to a person's day. Cumulatively, however, they are a huge drag on the organization.

For instance, is it really necessary to proof three drafts of a marketing mailing for the independent plumbing suppliers? Or was the second draft good enough for this shrinking market? What could your team members be doing with this time instead? This task may only take 10 minutes of a team member's day, but cut that, along with dozens of other small tasks that could be removed, and you've freed up a few hours for your team member to work on other projects, like updating your company's website with new materials to bring in prospective customers.

Each member of your team should be encouraged to spot and remove these items—and replace them with higher-value work. If there's a clear set of group priorities, this can happen naturally. If you assign someone a new high-profile project, they'll prioritize it and instinctively remove lower-priority items from their to-do list to make room for it. But it also helps if you can encourage and validate this trimming-back process. Make it clear that because you are adding higher-priority work for the group, you expect that existing work will need to be reshaped, delegated, or discarded to accommodate the new objective. When team members understand and internalize the group's priorities, they can use those priorities as a lens to examine their own work and make necessary cuts.

This process won't be perfect. By actively adding high-value priorities and shedding lower-value items to make room for the new work, at some point you or your team members will make a mistake. One of those low-value tasks will turn out to have more value than you thought and will need to be restarted. When this happens, don't abandon the new process or blame the employee. Add back that work, and acknowledge its medium value. If you discover that some people are making too many calls that backfire, have in-depth discussions with them about how they are prioritizing their to-do list. On the other hand, if you see that no one on your team makes any mistakes, it's probably a sign that they aren't pushing the process hard enough.

The goal here is to be nimble and flexible at all levels and to move the organization toward the future. Leaving the past behind requires that you put aside your natural biases and require that all objectives and projects prove their value. By actively identifying and weeding out Box 2 items—and encouraging your team to do the same—you can be assured that the priorities you're working toward offer the most value to your business.

———————

Jessica Avery is the Director of Business Analytics and Insights of the Harvard Business Review Group.

CHAPTER 18

What to Do When Strategic Goals Conflict

by Ron Ashkenas and Brook Manville

Strategy is the practice of translating your organization's vision and purpose into a set of specific goals, and then developing plans and actions to achieve them. As such, strategy is all about choices—what to do and what not to do; where to invest and where to pull back; how fast or slowly to proceed; how much risk to take.

On paper, this looks like a rational and straightforward process—just lay out the possible goals and plans, analyze the pros and cons, and make your decisions. The reality, however, is far messier. Sometimes the goals that emerge will require resources and skills that don't exist on your team; at other times the various goals—each of which makes sense on its own—conflict with each other and can't all be done. So what do you do?

To strike the right balance, you need an *execution strategy*. You need to assess carefully how you plan to follow through on the goals—whether that means making adjustments, finding necessary resources, or dropping priorities entirely. This chapter aims to show you how to ask the right questions of strategic goals so you can navigate through strategic tensions and find the right path forward.

Restarting Growth in a Competitive Market

Consider this example: A technology firm with a unique product had grown rapidly in its first 10 years from a startup to a $500 million business, but now it was hitting the wall. Competitors had entered its market, selling similar but lower-quality products at lower prices. To maintain its existing customer base, the technology firm had matched its competitors' prices, but now margins were shrinking and profitability was being squeezed.

In response to this changing financial landscape, the leadership team conducted a strategic analysis to identify ways of restarting its growth and regaining its place in the market. Three goals emerged:

- To dramatically reduce operating costs, lower prices, and win back market share

- To enhance the core product so that it would be more valuable for customers and therefore command a higher price

- To redirect its sales team toward larger enterprise customers who would pay a premium for quality

Unfortunately, these choices seemed mutually exclusive—or at least difficult to do simultaneously. If costs were significantly reduced, the company wouldn't have the resources or management bandwidth to focus on product enhancements or new go-to-market approaches. The company also didn't have the right talent to make these shifts, so it would require new investments, which weren't available unless the operating costs came down.

After much debate, the leadership team realized that looking at each goal individually was the wrong approach. Instead, they needed to look at each goal as part of a bigger picture. In doing so, they were able to create a path forward that allowed them to take on all three goals, but at different degrees of intensity.

First, they decided to go all-in on cost reduction and aimed to reduce operating expenses by 15% as quickly as possible. They knew that this would be painful and that they would lose some good talent—but they also felt that they had to generate profits that could be reinvested in the other two goals.

At the same time, however, they didn't want to wait six to twelve months for the product and sales shifts. To get those started, the head of R&D immediately canceled a number of longer-term and more speculative projects, and redeployed some of the engineers to a product-enhancement skunk works team. The team's specific challenge was to find ways of increasing the value of the company's technology for its customers and to test the most promising opportunities with several existing customers within three months.

Similarly, while reducing other operating costs, the head of sales asked three of his top performers to talk to a few large, high-end enterprises about their needs and how the company's technology could be helpful. They aimed to gain insights quickly so they could use that information to form the basis of a pilot go-to-market approach for large enterprises that could be tested in a few months.

Taking these steps did indeed help the company restart its growth, and this example illustrates an important point: The goals that emerge from your strategy should not be implemented piecemeal, but instead need to be considered holistically, as part of an overall execution strategy. If the goals are not part of an integrated plan, they might be pursued in the wrong sequence, cancel each other out, or receive less attention and fewer resources than they require.

Creating a Strategy Around Strategy

Though strategy is usually made at the highest level of a company, many executional choices may fall to you as a middle manager or unit team leader. As you develop the "strategy for the strategy," you must assess and communicate to senior leaders specific implementation issues related to the choices you're making, especially since they may not be as close to relevant frontline details as you are.

Voice your perspectives objectively and avoid being seen simply as a "naysayer"; if there are key implementation issues that have surfaced or hidden barriers to overcome, discuss them openly but constructively, suggesting ways to address them. Your goal is to help final decision makers detail an overall solution, ensuring the best possible choices and follow-through of what's being prioritized and sequenced.

Ask yourself the following questions when you are developing a "conflicting goal" execution strategy:

- **Sequencing.** Can you work on all of the strategic goals at the same time? If not, what needs to be tackled first? Are there resources or knowledge that can be gained from an early opportunity that could help another objective later? In our technology company case, for example, the team realized that they had to become cost competitive in order to remain financially viable, so changing the underlying operating model was a priority. In addition, the savings generated from this goal could then be reinvested in the other shifts later.

- **Bandwidth.** How much can you and your team do at once? Do you have the resources to focus on more than one major strategic project at a time? What will it take to keep the current business going while you are driving new strategic initiatives? In the example, the team at the technology firm decided that they didn't have either the resources or the management attention to do everything. But they could proceed on a couple of the goals if they carved them down to a much smaller scale, leading them to create a technology skunk works team and begin focused dialogue with potential higher-end customers.

- **Talent.** Do you have people in place that have the skills and know-how to move into new strategic territory? Will you need to hire new people or train existing staff? What's the extent of this investment, and how will it be integrated with the current team? Assess what your team or department brings to the strategy, and fill in any missing pieces. In the technology company, the leadership team realized that the main talent deficit was probably in the sales area, since high-end selling requires more of a consultative approach, which was not in their wheelhouse. But before hiring new people or training current ones (both of which can be costly), they decided to learn more about these customers so that their eventual investment would have a better chance of success.

- **Conflict resolution and rebalancing.** If the market or our resources change during planning, should our original assumptions about how to compete still prevail? Have our investigations suggested specific learnings that would substantially alter those assumptions? Are there serious disagreements between key stakeholders about the execution strategy? What's the root cause of the opposition? Are skeptical colleagues raising legitimate concerns that might call for refashioning the way forward? Even with a clear framework for allocating resources to complementary strategic initiatives, market changes, learning, and (let's be honest) human disagreements may crop up. Work to resolve these conflicts, and be ready to rebalance initiatives if the conditions warrant it.

Considering these points will help you create a clear execution strategy to meet multiple objectives. Of course, no strategic plan remains static. As you move forward on the early initiatives, you'll learn what works and what doesn't, and what assumptions might need to be changed. You'll start to see whether early pilots need to be reconfigured, or what it will take to scale them. You'll better understand what your people are capable of doing, and where they will need help. You'll assess further investments and when to make them. And as you do all of this, you'll continue to massage and adjust the overall framework based on everything you learn.

Strategic analysis and thinking almost always lead to a number of different goals, some of which might seem incompatible with others. Putting them together into an integrated implementation framework gives you a way of moving them forward, and learning as you go.

———————

Ron Ashkenas is an Emeritus Partner with Schaffer Consulting, a frequent contributor to *Harvard Business Review*, and the author or coauthor of four books on organizational transformation. He has worked with hundreds of managers over the years to help them translate strategy into action. **Brook Manville** is Principal of Brook Manville, LLC, a consultancy focused on strategy, organizational development, and executive leadership. A former partner of McKinsey & Company, he is a regular writer on leadership topics and coauthor of two books with Harvard Business Review Press. They are the co-authors of *Harvard Business Review Leader's Handbook* (Harvard Business Review Press, 2018). This article is based on research for that book.

CHAPTER 19

Assess and Manage Trade-Offs

Even with clearly set priorities and a well-defined execution strategy, plans are naturally subject to change in the course of business. Consider the team working on a new product that is suddenly asked to speed up production to satisfy the needs of a major customer. Or the request to add new features to an app, when the development budget is almost maxed out. Deciding whether to adjust course on key objectives requires careful thought, and you'll need to weigh the advantages and disadvantages of making a change. You need to manage trade-offs.

Making trade-offs involves understanding the real impact of your choice for your team, other departments, and the organization overall. Just because someone

---

Adapted from *Pocket Mentor: Thinking Strategically* (product #13281), Harvard Business Press, 2010.

makes a request that affects your team's priorities doesn't mean that you have to take action. In assessing trade-offs, you can decide whether your team can feasibly adjust their workload, whether it's in the best interest of the organization, and how to move forward if the requested action is, in fact, worth pursuing.

The following practices can you help you navigate through this difficult terrain.

List Pros and Cons

When you're facing a change to your priorities—a new strategy for your group, an additional product to market and sell, a shortened development time line—first consider what alternatives you have. You may have only one option to meet the new objective, or you may have many. For each potential course of action, ask yourself what advantages and disadvantages might be associated with that plan.

Consider a manager who was recently asked to design a new feature for a product on a tight deadline. His team is unlikely meet every strategic objective—develop the new product feature that doesn't threaten sales of earlier product versions, that can be sold at a sufficiently high price, avoids expensive redesign, and so forth. To see the trade-offs visually, he wrote down his list of pros and cons of adding the new feature. Table 19-1 shows how he conducted this assessment.

To create your own list, consider your company's and unit's strategic goals. Do these goals emphasize reducing costs? Improving brand awareness? Simplifying product-development processes? Asking these questions

TABLE 19-1

Pros and cons of a new product feature

Advantages	Disadvantages
• Allows us to charge a higher price to customers	• Might cannibalize sales of the previous product version
• Could attract new customer segments	• Could be perceived as unnecessary or a nuisance by consumers
• Might improve brand awareness; our company could be seen as on the leading edge of technology	• Would require expensive redesign of the base product

keeps organizational objectives front of mind as you consider alternatives. Your answers can help guide your decisions about what's okay to trade off—and what isn't—based on larger strategic objectives.

Your list doesn't need to be long or detailed, but it should provide enough bullet points for you to understand what this change would be contributing to your team and organization, and what you'd be risking by moving in this direction.

Assess Short- and Long-Term Outcomes

Next, think through the potential short- and long-term impacts of potential courses of action. For example, suppose you're wondering whether to cut prices on a product line that has experienced declining sales. You realize that adjusting prices in this way may boost sales this month or even this year. In the long run, however, this move could hurt revenue if consumers came to expect deep discounts on your company's offerings. They may hold off purchasing your products until you provide another discount.

In order to think strategically about short- and long-term impacts, consider these steps:

1. Meet with your boss to determine how much time you and your team should be allocating toward short-term issues versus long-term goals.

2. Review the work that you and your team have done in the past month to determine what has been accomplished on both short- and long-term issues. If the balance is not aligned with your group's priorities, set new guidelines for how your team spends its time.

3. Keep an ongoing log to determine how you and your team are spending your time. Every two weeks, evaluate whether you are giving the proper time and attention to short-term requirements and long-term goals. Readjust your focus if necessary.

4. When you face competing priorities, determine which are the most important and make those your first priority. When an urgent matter arises, determine how it fits into your daily plan and act accordingly.

5. Involve your team in decisions about how to make progress on long-term goals while addressing short-term needs. They may have a perspective on how to balance large objectives while still meeting immediate deadlines.

After a conversation with your boss and tracking your team's work, you may discover that while a lot of team time and attention may be spent on this declining product line, your overall goal is to increase sales across all products for the year. You may then decide that a price cut for this line makes sense to boost sales in the short-term, since you can also test how the product performs at this lower price. While this experiment is taking place, your team can turn its attention to other products in an effort to increase their sales and ensure the company's long-term growth.

Balance Unit and Company Needs

Some decisions involve trade-offs between your department or group and the company overall. Suppose you lead a sales group whose representatives have won numerous new accounts by promising customers early delivery dates on a new product. That's great for your group. But it puts a burden on product development, manufacturing, order processing, and customer service—all of which must accelerate their processes in order to meet the promises your sales reps have made.

This situation may lead to several possible outcomes. For example, forcing product development to release a product early may jeopardize the quality of the product. This, in turn, might affect that unit's strategic goal of raising the quality standard of all products. It may also cause a high volume of calls to customer service as users of the product complain about defects. Individuals in this department will be focusing more time on pacifying customers, rather than their own critical priorities. Your

167

promise of early delivery could thus hurt relationships with other groups within the company and with long-standing, existing customers.

In this case, you need to consider whether to trade-off some new sales in return for smoother operation of the rest of your company's functions, so your organization can serve all its customers, not just the newest ones. Always think about how changes to planned priorities may affect not only your group but others in the company as well.

Make the Final Decision

By taking these points into account, you can fully assess how to proceed when your priorities or plans change. (The box "Six Questions for Making Trade-Offs" provides a reminder of key questions to keep in mind as you make your decision.) Thinking through each of these considerations will help you realize what is most important to continue doing, and what trade-offs don't line up with your organization's strategic priorities.

It's worth noting, though, that sometimes making a trade-off requires nothing more than specifying what you *won't* do. For example, suppose your group is evaluating the possibility of creating tiered versions of a product—high-end, midmarket, and low-end. Your work throughout this process has revealed especially significant risks for low-end products: these offerings could hurt brand image and generate lower profits, neither of which align with company objectives. In this case, simply say no and explain your decision: "I don't know what

SIX QUESTIONS FOR MAKING TRADE-OFFS

1. What are your choices regarding the issue you're facing?

2. What are the pros and cons of each choice?

3. What are the potential short- and long-term ramifications of your choices?

4. How might knowledge of your company's or unit's strategic goals inform your decision?

5. What cross-functional effects should you consider while making your decision?

6. Taking all of your responses into account, what trade-off seems most appropriate to make in this situation?

a high-end version of the product would look like. But I do know that we won't do a low-end version. It'll damage our brand image, and it won't generate enough profit to justify production."

By defining trade-offs in this way, you help your group focus on the acceptable courses of action—and determine where a change may hurt your team, other departments, or the company overall. By keeping the organization's strategy front of mind, you can determine when and how to change course when the opportunity presents itself.

Align Your Team Around Strategic Goals

CHAPTER 20

To Be a Strategic Leader, Ask the Right Questions

by Lisa Lai

Strategy is complex. Thought leaders all over the world have created sophisticated frameworks designed to help leaders grapple with their own strategies at an abstract level. But the reality is that strategy succeeds or fails based on how well leaders at every level of an organization integrate strategic thinking into day-to-day operations. This is less about complexity and more about practical focus.

How can you personally be more strategic as a leader? Ask yourself and your team the five questions below to

Adapted from "Being a Strategic Leader Is About Asking the Right Questions" on hbr.org, January 18, 2017 (product #H03ENN).

drive clarity, alignment, and strategic insight. The questions build on one another, leading to a well-aligned, strategic perspective. If you make these five questions part of your ongoing dialogue, you will inevitably become more strategic and more successful as a team.

1. What Are We Doing Today?

Leaders are often surprised at just how much they don't know about what team members are working on. Here's why: Over time, organizations add more and more to the plates of various teams and employees. While leaders and team members talk at length about new initiatives and assignments, they focus less on legacy work that's still being done. At some point, leaders lose sight of just how much time people are investing in legacy priorities. Asking this question almost always brings to light significant work that managers aren't aware is being done or that's taking much more time than it should. You can't move your team forward strategically without knowing the answer to this question with total clarity.

2. Why Are We Doing the Work We're Doing? Why Now?

Once you've taken stock of all the work being done by your team, the next logical step is to examine the importance of that work. This serves two strategic purposes. First, you gain clarity on what's important and why it's important from your team's perspective. You'll likely uncover situations where you and your team are uncertain or in disagreement. This drives important conversations with your team about choices, resources, and trade-offs.

Second, you have the opportunity to attach value and meaning to the work your team is doing. Everyone wants to believe that the work they do matters. It's your job to understand and articulate that with your own team and across the organization. The only way you get there is with scrutiny.

3. How Does What We're Doing Today Align with the Bigger Picture?

Never underestimate the power of gaining total clarity about your own area of responsibility and then examining how well your work aligns with the broader goals of the organization. This is a discussion about gaps and outliers. If your team is working on something that doesn't align with the broader purpose or goals of the organization, you have a responsibility to challenge the value of doing that work. This is true even if your team believes the work is important or meaningful. Does it bring value to your customers? Does it contribute to the highest priorities of the business? Work that benefits both your customers and your business should be the top priority, and work that is no longer adding value should be removed (see chapter 17 for tips on how to do this). If you identify gaps that are not currently being addressed, more strategic discussion is needed. Are you doing exactly, and only, what most benefits your organization?

4. What Does Success Look Like for Our Team?

Chances are that you have a handful of measures that others use to evaluate your success. Do they tell the story of what success really looks like for your team? If you asked your team what success looks like for them individually and for the team overall, could they articulate an answer? The best strategic thinkers invest time here—not in trying to pacify their boss with a few measures that can readily be achieved, but in trying to understand what really drives success in terms of activities, behaviors, relationships, and strategic outcomes. The better you are able to align your team around a strong vision of success, the more likely you are to achieve it.

5. What Else Could We Do to Achieve More, Better, Faster?

Most leaders want to demonstrate their ability to "be strategic" by jumping directly to this question. If you haven't done the work to answer the preceding questions, it almost doesn't matter what you come up with here, because you may or may not be able to act on it. But if you have answered these questions, you are well positioned to be strategic in answering this one. You may identify new and better ways to serve the broader goals of your company. You may choose to redirect resources from current work that is relatively less important when compared to other new possibilities. This question is the most important of the five; every great leader needs to challenge their team to do more, better, or faster over time. It is, however, inextricably linked to the previous questions if you want to generate the best strategic insights.

Being a strategic leader is about asking the right questions and driving the right dialogue with your team. In doing so, you raise the team's collective ability to be strategic. The more competent you become in asking these questions, the better positioned you are to drive progress for your team and your organization.

Lisa Lai is an adviser, consultant, and coach for some of the world's most successful leaders and companies. She is also a moderator of global leadership development programs for Harvard Business School Publishing. Find her on Facebook, visit her website at www.laiventures .com, or follow her on Twitter @soul4breakfast.

CHAPTER 21

An Exercise to Get Your Team Thinking Differently About the Future

by Leonard M. Fuld

Thinking about the future is hard, mainly because we are glued to the present. Daniel Kahneman, the Nobel Prize–winning economist and author of *Thinking, Fast and Slow*, observed that decision makers get stuck in a memory loop and can only predict the future as a

Adapted from "An Exercise to Get Your Team Thinking Differently About the Future" on hbr.org, January 23, 2015 (product #H01TY2).

reflection of the past. He labels this dynamic the *narrative fallacy*—you see the future as merely a slight variation on yesterday's news. A way around this fallacy, we've found, is a speed-dating version of scenario planning, one that takes hours rather than months.

Consider the experiment we recently ran with an expert panel to jump-start fresh thinking about the future. Our guinea pigs consisted of life sciences executives from big pharma, biotech entrepreneurs, and academics.

The question we asked: *How might a shortage of science, technical, engineering, and math (STEM) talent affect the growth of life sciences companies?* The high-speed scenario workshop involved three steps:

1. Identify key story elements or drivers of the STEM talent "story" to be explored.

2. Conceive a plausible future by combining the elements.

3. Explore this future to understand its implications for their businesses.

Participants chose three drivers—forces that could be expected to shape the future of the life science industries: science education, federal investment in life sciences, and private investment. They then identified extremes for each driver that were far from their current state. For example, the group defined the education driver as "the degree to which U.S. elementary through higher education has developed curricula to produce science and technical talent." Participants decided that in their future story, the U.S. education system would substantially weaken, resulting in relatively few new science graduates, and that government funding, the second driver, would drop precipitously. Meanwhile, the group suggested that large-scale private investment in life sciences would soar.

Building a scenario based on the imagined future state of these drivers, the experts painted a picture of a world in which investor-funded technology companies would transform the traditional life sciences industry. In this world, life sciences research draws more on big-data analytics than lab-bench experiments, and virtual talent easily supplants large pools of scientists married to one location. The result is a more efficient and cost-effective industry.

By helping the group break free of the narrative fallacy, the exercise allowed them to rapidly build a scenario that stood in sharp contrast to their initial assumptions about the future—that a science-graduate shortage could only harm their industry.

Next, we asked participants to consider the strategic implications of this single future story. Here are a few of the provocative ideas the group advanced:

- Pharmaceutical and biotech firms will make smaller bets, and more of them. Private money, not government grants, will fuel these bets.

- There will be more R&D partnerships between private organizations like the Gates Foundation and biotech firms, as well as big pharma. Private foundations will supplement, but not replace, anemic government funding.

- Crowdsourcing will become a fundamental R&D engine. This will allow corporations to continue to pursue R&D near current levels but at lower cost.

- Big data and analytics companies such as Google will reshape life sciences R&D, shifting the emphasis from hands-on laboratory experimentation to virtual research facilitated by ever-increasing computing power.

While a two-hour exercise could never substitute for a full-bore, months-long scenario planning activity, our experiment did get participants out of their usual frame of reference, opening their eyes to a possible future that would require very different types of investment and research. That this shift can happen in a matter of hours shows how workshops like this one can unstick executive thinking.

To make exercises like this work, a disciplined facilitator must prepare and guide the participants. They don't need to be given a formal write-up, but relevant research materials must be handy (in our case, these included a handful of short articles on life sciences growth trends, as well as a few news reports on STEM talent); and the facilitator must serve as an editor, pruning and clarifying the flood of ideas the group will generate. Given the tight constraints on such exercises, the facilitator has to carefully balance the time devoted to imagining a future world, and to "living" in it—that is, exploring how the envisioned future might actually affect participants' businesses and industry.

Obviously, a brief workshop like this one shouldn't be used to shape strategy; that requires true scenario planning. But we've found that such exercises work well to dislodge narrow thinking about the future, neutralize Kahneman's narrative fallacy, and kick-start a strategy conversation with your team.

————————

Leonard M. Fuld is president of LMF Services and founder and CEO of Fuld + Company, a global consultancy providing competitive insights through its research and advisory services. His most recent book is *The Secret Language of Competitive Intelligence.*

CHAPTER 22

Communicating a Corporate Vision to Your Team

by Kelly Decker and Ben Decker

A manager we'll call Amit supervises a team of 40 people around the globe for a massive tech company. After his team spent months furiously working on a new product to be the first to market, Amit's boss told him that the company's strategy had shifted. The product's launch plans were then delayed, and competitors began gobbling up market share. The team felt deflated. Instead of celebrating a launch, they found themselves mired in more contract negotiations, tactical challenges, and

---

Adapted from "Communicating a Corporate Vision to Your Team" on hbr.org, July 10, 2015 (product #H026YB).

follow-up calls. They doubted the new strategy. Amit had to restore their trust and motivation. He needed to communicate vision.

Let's clear something up. Amit's big task was not to *set* the vision. In this case, the product strategy had changed at the top. His job was to translate the executives' thinking behind the changes, so his team could understand *why* things had changed and *how* they were supposed to redirect their efforts. After all, they were now being told to scrap all the work they'd done, go back to the drawing board, and renegotiate every painstaking contract. Without clarity around the *why* and *how*, it would be hard for them to execute the new strategy.

There are two things to remember when trying to communicate an organizational vision to your team. First, target your message. A team in IT has different needs than a team in marketing. Leaders are responsible for translating the same vision into different messages that their unique teams will respond to. Second, augment logical reasoning with an emotional appeal to inspire. That's how you get buy-in, and how you shift the team's response from "I have to" to "I want to."

We've developed a communication approach that breaks this down into four key components to be addressed: listeners, point of view, actions, and benefits.

Understand Your Listeners

Step back and think about your team. Sure, you know the player roster well, but attitudes change over time (e.g., from the beginning of a project to the end). Before you start on the vision, take a few minutes to answer the following questions about your team:

- What do they know about the current status of your project or goal or bigger strategy? What are they expecting? How do they feel about the team and the organization right now?

- How would they challenge the vision? What would make them resistant?

- How can I help them? What problems am I trying to solve that will make their lives better in some way?

Find the Lede of Your Story

With the broader vision in mind, it's time to develop the specific point of view for your team. Think of this as the *why* behind the message. What is the one thing that you want everyone to walk away knowing? Don't get too granular or tactical. You're simply looking for a motivator—some way to get the team to nod their heads and accept the change.

For his team, Amit couldn't default to something as narrow as, "We need to negotiate new contracts for the new changes to our product." Yes, that was a key element (and it needed motivation!), but that wasn't an inspiring vision. Instead, he had to make it bigger: "Our current product faced a massive risk of being commoditized. Our products have never been commodities! We must always position ourselves as the leader in this space."

Point the Way

After you have developed your point of view, it's time to zero in on your next challenge: converting vision into action—or pointing your team in the right direction so they can make something happen. You don't have to lay out every step that leads to your ultimate goal, but you do have to be specific and set benchmarks and deadlines. Action steps have to be physical, timed, and measurable to pave a way toward the vision that the team can actually see. For instance, Amit's team had much work to complete over the next quarter. To get them started on renegotiating the contracts immediately, he asked each of them to schedule meetings with three key stakeholders by the end of the week.

Give Them a Reason to Believe

To get your team behind the vision, your message also has to address what's in it for them—each of them. Too often we provide a laundry list of general benefits that are far too removed from people's real-life situations to really motivate anyone. Better ROI, increased top-line growth, and greater customer satisfaction are all great for the organization—they just don't mean that much to us as individuals. Team leaders have to drive the benefit down to the individual level as much as possible. The best way to do this is to connect the dots. Go back to how you described your team. Amit could appeal to his team's pride in leading the industry, or the accolades they would add to their professional trophy cases: "Look at what you'll create." This individual focus engages people's emotions and moves them to action. After all, logic makes us think; emotion drives us to act.

Emotion can also come from analogies, stories, or concrete examples that illustrate what success looks like. As Chip and Dan Heath describe in their book *Switch*, you want to create a destination postcard, or "a vivid picture from the near-term future that shows what could be possible." Describe exactly what success will look like for your team, so everyone envisions the same goal. They should reach the same answers for questions like: *How will customers feel when they use the product? What will the analysts say? How about kudos from the top? What do the ratings and reviews show?*

In order to get his team's buy-in, Amit had to be more transparent about why the company was shifting to the new plan. He also had to demonstrate that he was listening. So he explained how individual strengths and contributions from team members would move them forward. This approach helped Amit's team feel once again proud and invested. The change in morale was noticeable across emails and check-ins. The team started rebuilding momentum. (The box "How to Communicate an Organizational Vision to Your Team" highlights example language Amit used to motivate his team at the tech company.)

As a team leader, you're not always the one to set the grand overarching vision, but your role—communicating it and casting it in a way that motivates your team—is essential. Getting your team to see how their work matters

HOW TO COMMUNICATE AN ORGANIZATIONAL VISION TO YOUR TEAM

Four Steps to Move Them to Action

New company vision example: "We're shifting our focus to the cloud instead of developing separate services for each client."

1. *Think about your audience.* What do they care most about? *"Your product development team cares about the end result; they want to be proud of the product they built."*

2. *Target the message to their needs.* How is the vision relevant to them? *"Our goal is to always be industry leaders. A cloud-based service is a better way of achieving that."*

3. *Lay out action steps.* What are specific, measurable goals and deadlines? *"Our first major task is to meet with our key stakeholders and get their input on the new design by the end of the next week."*

4. *Engage their emotions.* How will they benefit at the end? *"This will streamline a lot of your future work, and your name will be forever tied to the success of this project."*

Source: Ben Decker and Kelly Decker, *Communicate to Influence* (McGraw-Hill Education, 2015).

on an organizational level will keep them motivated and productive, especially during times of change. It will also reflect well on you as their manager. That's the value of the vision.

———————

Kelly Decker and **Ben Decker** are leading experts in the field of business communication. They run Decker Communications, a global firm that trains and coaches tens of thousands of executives a year. They are the coauthors of *Communicate to Influence: How to Inspire Your Audience to Action*, which shares real-world stories and tips from the C-suite that apply to us all.

Move from Thinking Strategically to Executing the Strategy

CHAPTER 23

Execution Is a People Problem, Not a Strategy Problem

by Peter Bregman

Paul, the CEO of Maxreed, a global publishing company, was having trouble sleeping. (Names and some details in this story have been changed to protect privacy.) Publishing is an industry that's changing even faster than most other fast-changing industries, but Paul wasn't awake worrying about his strategy. He had a solid plan that took advantage of new technologies, and the board

---

Adapted from "Execution Is a People Problem, Not a Strategy Problem" on hbr.org, January 4, 2017 (product #H03DWS).

and his leadership team were aligned around it. Paul and his team had already reorganized the structure—new divisions, revised roles, redesigned processes—to support their strategy.

So what was Paul worrying about? People.

Which is precisely what he *should* be worrying about. However hard it is to devise a smart strategy, it's 10 times harder to get people to execute on that strategy. And a poorly executed strategy, no matter how clever, is worthless.

In other words, your organization's biggest strategic challenge isn't strategic thinking—it's *strategic acting*.

You need to get your people working together in the same strategic direction. If I were to depict the challenge graphically, it would be going from figure 23-1a, where the employees are working in different directions, targeting different priorities, to figure 23-1b, where employees are aligned and heading toward the same objective—what I call "the Big Arrow."

The conundrum is how to get from the first graphic to the second one. Most organizations rely on communication plans to make that shift. Unfortunately, strategy *communication*, even if you do it daily, is not the same as—and is not enough to drive—strategy *execution*. Because while strategy development and communication are about *knowing* something, strategy execution is about *doing* something. And the gap between what you know and what you do is often huge. Add in the necessity of having everyone acting in alignment with each other, and it gets even bigger.

FIGURE 23-1

The Big Arrow

Move from (a) to (b) to align your team with the most important work that drives strategy.

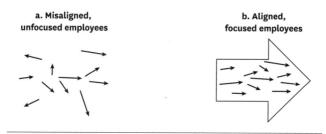

a. Misaligned, unfocused employees

b. Aligned, focused employees

The reason strategy execution is often glossed over by even the most astute strategy consultants is because primarily it's not a strategy challenge. It's a human behavior one.

To deliver stellar results, people need to be hyper-aligned and laser-focused on the highest-impact actions that will drive the organization's most important outcomes. But even in well-run, stable organizations, people are misaligned, too broadly focused, and working at cross-purposes.

Aligning people isn't critical only for a changing company in a changing industry like Paul's. It's also imperative for fast-growing startups. And companies in turnaround situations. And those with new leadership. Any time it's critical to focus on strategy—and when isn't it?—the most important strategy question you need to answer is: *How can we align everyone's efforts and help them accomplish the organization's most important work?*

That's the question Paul reached out to ask me. Below is the solution we implemented with him at Maxreed. This is the Big Arrow process, and it represents my best thinking after 25 years of experimenting with this very challenge.

Define the Big Arrow

We worked with Paul and a small group of his leaders to identify the most important outcome for Maxreed to achieve over the following 12 months. Their Big Arrow had to do with creating a strategy and product roadmap that was supported by the entire leadership team. The hardest part of this is getting to that *one* most important thing, the thing that would be a catalyst for driving the rest of the strategy forward.

Once we defined the Big Arrow, we tested it with a series of questions. If you answer yes to each of these questions, it's likely that your Big Arrow is on target:

- Will success in the Big Arrow drive the mission of the larger organization?

- Is the Big Arrow supporting, and supported by, your primary business goals?

- Will achieving it make a statement to the organization about what's most important?

- Will it lead to the execution of your strategy?

- Is it the appropriate stretch?

- Are you excited about it? Do you have an emotional connection to it?

Along with that outcome clarity, we also created behavioral clarity by identifying the most important behavior that would lead to achieving the outcome. For Maxreed, the behavior was about collaborating with trust and transparency. We determined this by asking one key question: *What current behavior do we see in the organization that will make driving the Big Arrow harder and make success less likely?* We then articulated the opposite, which became our Big Arrow behavior.

Identify the Highest-Impact People

Once the Big Arrow was clear, we worked with Paul and his HR partner to identify the people who were most essential to achieving the goal. Doing this is critical because you want to focus your efforts and resources on the people who will have the most impact on the Big Arrow. In the case of Maxreed, we identified 10 people whose roles were core to the project, who already had organizational authority, and who were highly networked. With other clients, we've identified many more people at all levels of the hierarchy. As you think about who might be the appropriate people, ask the questions: *Who has the greatest capacity to affect the forward momentum of the arrow? Who is an influencer in the organization? Who has an outsize impact on our Big Arrow outcome or behavior?* Those are the people you should choose.

Determine What They Should Focus On

Once we established the key people, we worked with each of them and their managers to determine their:

- Key contribution to moving the Big Arrow forward

- Pivotal strength that will allow them to make their key contribution

- Game changer—the thing that, if the person improves, will most improve their ability to make their key contribution

One of the things that makes this process successful is its simplicity. It's why we settled on *one* pivotal strength and *one* most critical game changer. Strategy execution needs to be laser-focused, and one of the biggest impediments to forward momentum on our most important work is trying to get forward momentum on *all* our work. Simplicity requires that we make choices. What will have the biggest impact? Then we make that one thing happen.

Hold Laser-Focused Coaching Sessions

Once we made sure the right people had the right focus, we coached in laser-focused, 30-minute one-on-one coaching sessions. Coaching is often used in organizations to fix a leader's flaws, but that is not the focus of this kind of coaching. Here, individuals were coached to focus on making clear headway on their key contribution to the Big Arrow. These conversations only focus on larger behavioral patterns to the extent that they are getting in the way of the task at hand.

Collect and Share Data

Because we were coaching multiple people, we were able to maintain strict confidentiality with the individuals being coached while collecting data about trends and organizational obstacles they were facing, which we reported to Paul and his leadership team. This wasn't just opinion survey data; it represented the real obstacles preventing Maxreed's most valuable people from driving the company's most important priorities forward.

One of the main challenges we uncovered was a lack of cross-functional collaboration. Armed with that insight, Paul was able to address this issue directly, getting the key people in a room together and speaking openly about the issue. Eventually, he initiated a new cross-functional Big Arrow process that included leaders from the groups that weren't collaborating. Identifying what they needed to achieve together broke down the walls between the groups.

Amplify Performance

While Paul removed organizational obstacles, coaches continued to help Maxreed's most critical people tackle the particular obstacles and challenges they faced as they delivered their key contribution. Coaches addressed the typical challenges people struggle with when executing strategy: how to communicate priorities, how to deal with someone who is resistant, how to influence someone who doesn't report to you, how to say no to distractions, and so on. The coaching prioritized helping people build relationships on their own teams and across silos, which was supported by the data and the Big Arrow key behavior of collaborating with trust and transparency. Individuals aligned with the goals of the organization to drive continued growth and success.

While the Big Arrow process was ongoing, we sent out a survey to people being coached as well as others outside the program to assess progress being made by the key contributors. Compared to before the coaching, are they more effective or less effective at making their key contribution, achieving the outcomes of the Big Arrow, and addressing their game changer? There were 98 responses to the survey:

Key contribution: 90% said either more effective or much more effective.

Big Arrow: 88% said either more effective or much more effective.

Game changer: 84% said either more effective or much more effective.

In other words, the key contributors were getting massive traction in moving the organization's most important work—its key strategy—forward. This data was confirmed by Paul's own observations of the progress they've made on their Big Arrow outcome, a strategy and product roadmap that is supported by the entire leadership team. Maybe most important, the broader organization was noticing. Which, of course, is how you start a movement.

Paul is still working hard to continue the momentum of the strategic shift. That's the point, really: Strategy execution is not a moment in time. It's thousands of moments across time. But now, at least, it's happening.

———————

Peter Bregman is CEO of Bregman Partners, a company that helps clients get massive traction on their most important work through the Big Arrow process and as a coach and adviser to CEOs and their leadership teams. He is the best-selling author of *18 Minutes*, and his most recent book is *Four Seconds*.

CHAPTER 24

How to Excel at Both Strategy and Execution

by Paul Leinwand and Joachim Rotering

For decades, we've often thought of leadership profiles in unique buckets—two popular varieties were the "visionaries," who embrace strategy and think about amazing things to do, and the "operators," who get stuff done. We intuitively knew that there must be leaders that span these areas, but in fact, few do. According to a global survey of 700 executives across a variety of industries conducted by Strategy&, the strategy consulting division of PwC, only 8% of company leaders were said to excel at both strategy and execution.

Adapted from "How to Excel at Both Strategy and Execution" on hbr .org, November 17, 2017 (product #H040X2).

You Can't Choose Strategy *or* Execution

You may think that success can be achieved by excelling at either strategy or execution individually—that great visionaries can change how we see the world, or that amazing operators can wind up outperforming competitors. But our experience and research suggest that the days of keeping strategy and execution as separate topics are ending: We need leaders who can make big promises to customers *and* help their organizations deliver on those promises.

Take Starbucks: CEO Howard Schultz created a very ambitious aspiration for the company, far more than just being a seller of coffee. He wanted Starbucks to be a "third place" for conviviality beyond home and the workplace. Visit a Starbucks anywhere in the world, and you will find the same consistently comfortable and welcoming ambiance. But he didn't get there simply by telling his staff to "be warm and friendly."

Starbucks has been able to deliver on its promise because that promise is tightly linked to the company's distinctive capabilities. The feel of Starbucks stores isn't created merely by the layout and the décor—it exists because the people behind the counter understand how their work fits into a common purpose, and recognize how to accomplish great things together without needing to follow a script.

Over many years, Starbucks has built a capability to foster a relationship-driven, "employees-first" approach. It was Schultz who famously said, "You can walk into [any type of retail store] and you can feel whether the proprietor or the merchant or the person behind the counter has a good feeling about his product. If you walk into a department store today, you are probably talking to a guy who is untrained; he was selling vacuum cleaners yesterday, and now he is in the apparel section. It just does not work."

Schultz made sure that Starbucks would be different: Workers are called "partners" rather than employees, and even part-time staff (in the United States) receive stock options and health insurance. At the height of the global financial crisis, when other companies were cutting HR costs wherever they could, Starbucks invested in staff training, including coffee tastings and courses that ultimately qualified employees for credit at higher education institutions. Beyond employees, much of what you will see and experience at Starbucks has been well thought out to accomplish the company's mission, from the music played to the furniture selected. Even the bathrooms are strategic at Starbucks, because they play a part in allowing customers to spend time in the "third place."

Leaders like Howard Schultz don't just have both the visionary and operator skills—they deeply value the connection between the two skill sets. They see them as inextricably linked, since a bold vision needs to include both a very ambitious destination *and* a well-conceived path for execution that will get you there. This is ever more important today, when differentiating your company is so difficult. Differentiation increasingly requires more innovative thinking and the use of very specific areas of expertise (like Apple's winning design, a capability that wouldn't have been prioritized in most technology companies before Steve Jobs did so).

Leaders who master both strategy and execution start by building a bold but executable strategy. Next, they ensure that the company is investing behind the change. And last, they make sure the entire organization is motivated to go the journey.

Ask What Your Company Is Already Great At

Developing a bold but executable strategy starts with making sure leaders have addressed the questions of "What are we great at?" and "What are we able to achieve?" rather than coming up with lofty plans and asking functional and business-unit teams to do their best to execute. Indeed, they spell out the few differentiating capabilities that the company must excel at to realize the strategy.

Ensuring that the company is investing behind the change means that leaders recognize that the budget process is one of the most important tools in closing the strategy-to-execution gap. Cost isn't an exogenous variable to be managed; it is the investment in doing the most important things well. But rarely are budgets linked closely to the strategy. If your company is merely incrementalizing the budget up or down by a few percentage points, ask yourself whether the investments really reflect the most important tasks.

Motivating individuals is a hugely underleveraged tool to close the gap between strategy and execution. Great leaders know that success stems from specific skills that come together in unique ways to do the challenging tasks in executing the strategy. But, today, most employees don't even understand how they are connected to the strategy. In a recent survey of 540 executives, managers, and nonmanagers by Strategy&, only 28% of employees said that they feel fully connected to the purpose and identity of their organization. Articulating the strategy in human terms—what capabilities the company will need to build and what skills are required to do so—not only helps the company focus on how to develop the right talent, but it allows individuals to understand how their role fits into the overall strategy and to see their work in a much more fundamentally connected way.

Questions for Bringing Together Strategy and Execution

How do you combine strategy and execution? Below are some questions to ask yourself that cover all three stages of the strategy-to-execution continuum. Getting these three areas right allows leaders to make a big step forward toward closing the gap between strategy and execution:

1. **Build the strategy.**

   - Are you very clear about how you add value to customers in a way that others don't, and about the specific capabilities that enable you to excel at that value proposition?

   - As strategies are being developed, are you using the classic approach of "build the strategy, then think about execution," or are you asking yourself the question, "Do you have the capabilities needed—or can you build the capabilities needed—to execute the strategy?"

- As you're dealing with disruption, are you shaping the world around you with your given strengths, or are you waiting for change to happen and therefore playing by someone else's rules?

2. **Translate the strategy into the everyday.**

- Are you diligently following through on what you have decided? You need to be very clear about what the strategy is and what it takes to succeed—and to communicate it so that everyone in the organization understands what they should be doing.

- Are there visible programs (for example, specific new technologies, new processes, or training programs) to build the key capabilities your organization needs to win with its strategy?

- Are you building specific connections between strategy and the budgeting process so you're reallocating funds to where they matter most? And do you have mechanisms in place that translate the strategy into personal goals and rewards for managers and employees?

3. **Execute the strategy.**

- Are you motivating employees every single day to understand how what they're doing connects to the important strategic levers that you have focused on?

- Are you enabling employees to work together across organizational silos to tackle the cross-functional challenges that allow the company to win?

- Are you keeping track not just of your performance, but of how you're building and scaling up those few key capabilities that enable you to create value for customers in ways that others cannot?

- Is your management team engaged in how you are executing the strategy, not just by measuring results, but by constantly challenging the organization and supporting it in improving its key capabilities? Are you setting your team's sights high enough for what they need to accomplish, and by when?

We believe there's a tremendous upside for companies that can succeed at strategy through execution. The leaders who are able to be both visionaries and operators, and switch between these two mindsets, are the ones who can turn their organizations into super-competitors.

———————

Paul Leinwand is Global Managing Director, Capabilities-Driven Strategy and Growth, with Strategy&, PwC's strategy consulting business. He is a principal with PwC U.S. He is also the coauthor of several books, including *Strategy That Works: How Winning Companies Close the Strategy-to-Execution Gap* (Harvard Business Review Press, 2016). **Joachim Rotering** is the Strategy& Global Leader as well as the Europe, Middle East, and Africa Leader. He is a Managing Director with PwC Strategy& (Germany) and works primarily with clients in the oil, chemicals, and steel industries.

CHAPTER 25

How the Most Successful Teams Bridge the Strategy-to-Execution Gap

by Nathan Wiita and Orla Leonard

The strategy-to-execution gap is an enduring problem with no easy solution. As the Japanese proverb goes, "Vision without action is a daydream. Action without vision is a nightmare." Paul Leinwand and his coauthors, in chapter 24 of this guide and elsewhere, have outlined what senior leaders must do to close the strategy-to-execution gap. We built on this research by going beyond

Adapted from "How the Most Successful Teams Bridge the Strategy-to-Execution Gap" on hbr.org, November 23, 2017 (product #H0414W).

the lens of the individual leader to investigate how the most successful teams bridge the gap. We wanted to unpack the *how* by identifying what sets these teams apart in terms of how they spend their time and the critical behaviors they engage in. To do this, we examined how 49 enterprise leadership teams spend their time and also looked at their perceived effectiveness on critical behaviors of a senior team. They also responded to items that corresponded to the Leinwand et al. framework, as detailed below.

Commit to an identity. The first tenet of their framework is that an organization must commit to an identity through a shared understanding of its value proposition and distinctive capabilities. In short, the organization must commit to focus on what it is good at and then go after it. We found that the key differentiators for high-performing teams are:

- They spend nearly 20% more time (compared to low-performing teams) defining strategy (i.e., translating a high-level vision into clear actionable goals).

- They spend 12% more time aligning the organization around that strategy through frequent internal communications and driving a consistent message downward into the organization.

Indeed, our experience with senior teams corroborates this data. That is, we've found that teams that excel in this arena are those that break strategy into clear, practical deliverables and then cascade those deliverables downward through frequent messaging.

Translate strategy into everyday processes and capabilities. Our analysis of how senior teams spend their time shows that, for this dimension:

- High-performing teams spend over 25% more time focusing the enterprise than their lower-performing peers. That time is spent establishing financial and operational metrics, aligning goals with overarching strategy, allocating resources, and reviewing key metrics.

- High-performing teams spend 14% more time checking their progress against strategic goals by reviewing key metrics and shifting resources accordingly.

The most successful senior teams create a permeable membrane between the organization's mission and its day-to-day activities. They are also agile in correcting course when the needs of the business change and are more easily prepared to shift organizational resources to ensure that the strategy is executed.

Concentrate on the unique cultural factors that fuel success. Implicit in this assumption is resisting the temptation to drive traditional change programs based on addressing gaps or weaknesses. This is an area where the data presents a more complex picture.

- High-performing teams spend 28% more time engaging the organization in ongoing dialogue about cultural enablers and barriers to execution. This includes forums for employees to voice concerns via surveys (for example, employee engagement) and actual dialogue.

- Those same teams invest almost one-third more time in optimizing talent capabilities by reviewing development plans, ensuring that succession plans are in place, and evaluating compensation plans to be competitive.

Our data suggests that the approach of leveraging cultural strengths is both commendable and efficient, but organizations that continue to monitor and challenge their cultural and leadership biases are those that have the edge. Simply focusing on strengths is not enough.

The academic literature as well as our consulting experience suggest that the ability to prioritize is a key ingredient to an enterprise leadership team's success. This is no small task, given the constant and overwhelming demands on most teams. What does our data suggest about *how* teams go about this?

- High-performing teams, compared to lower-performing teams, spend 54% more time first setting direction, crafting a vision that serves as a guiding light for decisions regarding resources.

- When it comes to execution, lower-performing teams spend an astounding 83% more time firefighting and dealing with issues at a tactical rather than strategic level.

Our high-performing teams in this dimension also rated themselves 36% more effective at prioritizing and sequencing initiatives than the lower-performing cohort. Our experience suggests that a critical piece in prioritization can be as simple as determining when the team comes together and what topics it discusses. Ensuring that the top team is sufficiently elevated and creating a consistent drumbeat around priorities will prevent distractions and cement the close link between strategy and execution.

Shape the future. High-performing teams successfully shape the future, rather than always being in a reactive mode in the present. How do they do it?

- They spend 25.3% more time influencing high-level stakeholders by identifying their needs and managing their expectations.

- Unsurprisingly, though easier said than done, the high-performing teams spend 13.2% more time planning for the future by setting direction, creating a vision, and defining their strategy.

- Finally, they shape the future by responding to change in the present (20.7% more effectively than lower-performing teams), positioning the enterprise for future success. This is consistent with much of the existing literature on the importance of agility in high-performing teams.

How might you close the strategy-to-execution gap in your own company? We believe that being intentional about the best and highest use of the team's time is the key lever in getting results.

Where should you start? As we look across our findings, teams that performed well across the strategy-to-execution dimensions did the following:

- Spent more time strategizing and translating that strategy into actionable goals

- Spent more time engaging the organization, surfacing barriers and unmet needs and communicating direction and behavioral guardrails

- Spent more time interacting with key stakeholders to ascertain and anticipate roadblocks and opportunities

- Spent less time fighting fires

Take a glance at the agendas of your team meetings over the last 6 to 12 months. Then, ask yourself the following questions:

- What percentage of the team's time was spent firefighting or dealing with issues that could have been dealt with at the next level down? How much time was invested on the big-ticket strategic items?

- How much time did the team spend thinking proactively about the future of our industry, our business model, the regulatory landscape, and our consumers?

- What percentage of time did the team spend engaging and aligning with the organization? How about key stakeholders? Does the team have a decent pulse check on its blatant and latent needs?

Perhaps most important, ask yourself, "Have we successfully executed our strategy?"

———————

Nathan Wiita is a Principal and Research and Innovation Lead at RHR International. **Orla Leonard** is a Partner and Practice Leader of Senior Team Effectiveness at RHR International.

CHAPTER 26

Get Your Team to Do What It Says It's Going to Do

by Heidi Grant

Say you're in the early stages of planning your department's budget for the next fiscal year. Your management team meets to establish short-term priorities and starts to think about longer-term resource allocation. You identify next steps and decide to reconvene in a week—but when you do, you find that very little progress has been made. What's the holdup? Your to-dos probably look something like this:

Step 1: Develop a tentative budget for continuing operations.

Reprinted from "Get Your Team to Do What It Says It's Going to Do" in *Harvard Business Review*, May 2014 (product #R1405E).

Step 2: Clarify the department's role in upcoming corporate initiatives.

Those steps may be logical, but they're ineffective because they omit essential details. Even the first one, which is relatively straightforward, raises more questions than it answers: What data must the team gather to estimate requirements for continuing operations? Who will run the reports, and when? Which managers can shed additional light on resource needs? Who will talk to them and reconcile their feedback with what the numbers say? When will that happen? Who will assess competing priorities and decide which trade-offs to make? When?

Creating goals that teams and organizations will actually accomplish isn't just a matter of defining what needs doing; you also have to spell out the specifics of getting it done, because you can't assume that everyone involved will know how to move from concept to delivery. By using what motivational scientists call *if-then planning* to express and implement your group's intentions, you can significantly improve execution.

If-then plans work because contingencies are built into our neurological wiring. Humans are very good at encoding information in "If x, then y" terms and using those connections (often unconsciously) to guide their behavior. When people decide exactly when, where, and how they will fulfill their goals, they create a link in their brains between a certain situation or cue ("If or when x happens") and the behavior that should follow ("then I will do y"). In this way, they establish powerful triggers for action.

We've learned from more than 200 studies that if-then planners are about 300% more likely than others to reach their goals. Most of that research focuses on individuals, but we're starting to uncover a similar effect in groups. Several recent studies indicate that if-then planning improves team performance by sharpening groups' focus and prompting members to carry out key activities in a timely manner.

That's an important finding, because organizations squander enormous amounts of time, money, ideas, and talent in pursuit of poorly expressed goals. If-then planning addresses that pervasive problem by sorting out the fine-grained particulars of execution for group members. It pinpoints conditions for success, increases everyone's sense of responsibility, and helps close the troublesome gap between knowing and doing.

Overcoming Obstacles to Execution

Peter Gollwitzer, the psychologist who first studied if-then planning (and my postdoctoral adviser at New York University), has described it as creating "instant habits." Unlike many of our other habits, these don't get in the way of our goals but help us reach them. Let's look at a simple work example.

Suppose your employees have been remiss in submitting weekly progress reports, and you ask them all to set the goal of keeping you better informed. Despite everyone's willingness, people are busy and still forget to do it. So you ask them each to make an if-then plan: "If it's 2 p.m. on Friday, I will email Susan a brief progress report."

Now the cue "2 p.m. on Friday" is directly wired in their brains to the action "email my report to Susan"—and it's just dying to get noticed. Below their conscious awareness, your employees begin to scan the environment for it. As a result, they will spot and seize the critical moment ("It's 2 p.m. on Friday") *even when they're busy doing other things.*

Once the "if" part of the plan is detected, the mind triggers the "then" part. People now begin to execute the plan without having to think about it. When the clock hits 2 on Friday afternoon, the hands automatically reach for the keyboard. Sometimes you're aware that you are following through. But the process doesn't have to be conscious, which means you and your employees can still move toward your goal while occupied with other projects.

This approach worked in controlled studies: Participants who created if-then plans submitted weekly reports only 1.5 hours late, on average. Those who didn't create them submitted reports eight hours late.

The if-then cue is really important—but so is specifying what each team member will do and when (and often where and how). Let's go back to the budgeting example. To make it easier for your team to execute the first step, developing a tentative budget for continuing operations, you might create if-then plans along these lines:

> *When it's Monday morning, Jane will detail our current expenses for personnel, contractors, and travel. If it's Monday through Wednesday, Surani and David*

will meet with the managers in their groups to get input on resource needs.

When it's Thursday morning, Phil will write a report that synthesizes the numbers and the qualitative feedback.

When it's Friday at 2 p.m., the management team will reassess priorities in light of Phil's report and agree on trade-offs.

Now there's less room for conflicting interpretations. The tasks and time frames are clearly outlined. Individuals know what they're accountable for, and so do the others in the group.

Does the if-then syntax feel awkward and stilted? It might, since it doesn't reflect the way we naturally express ourselves. But that's actually a good thing, because when we articulate our goals more "naturally," the all-important details of execution don't stick. The if-then construction makes people more aware and deliberate in their planning, so they not only understand but also complete the needed tasks.

Solving Problems That Plague Groups

Beyond helping managers get better results from their direct reports, if-then planning can address some of the classic challenges that groups face when working and making decisions together. Members often allow cognitive biases to obscure their collective judgment; for example, falling into traps such as groupthink and fixation on sunk costs. New findings suggest that if-then planning can offer effective solutions to this class of problems.

Groupthink

In theory, teams should be better decision makers than individuals, because they can benefit from the diverse knowledge and experience that each member brings. But they rarely capitalize on what each person distinctively has to offer. Rather than offering up unique data and insights, members focus on information that they all possess from the start. Many forces are at work here, but primary among them is the desire to reach consensus quickly and without conflict by limiting the discussion to what's familiar to everyone.

Even when team members are explicitly told to share all relevant information with one another—and have monetary incentives to do so—they still don't. When people are entrenched in existing habits, paralyzed by cognitive overload, or simply distracted, they tend to forget to execute general goals like this.

Research by J. Lukas Thürmer, Frank Wieber, and Peter Gollwitzer conducted at the University of Konstanz demonstrates how if-then plans improve organizational decision making through increased information exchange and cooperation. In their studies, teams worked on "hidden profile" problems—which required members to share knowledge to identify the best solution. For instance, in one study, three-person panels had to choose the best of three job applicants. Candidate A was modestly qualified, with six out of nine attributes in his favor—but every panel member knew about all six attributes. Candidate B also had six attributes in his favor, but every panel member knew about three of them, and each had unique knowledge of one additional attribute. Candidate C, the superior candidate, had nine out of nine attributes in his favor, but each panel member received information about only three attributes. To realize that Candidate C had all nine, the members of a panel had to share information with one another.

All the panels were instructed to do so before coming to a final decision and were told that reviewing the bottom two candidates' positive attributes would be a good way to accomplish this. Half the panels made an if-then plan: "If we are ready to make a decision, then we will review the positive qualities of the other candidates before deciding." (All study participants knew that the if-then plans applied specifically to them—and that the task needed to be done at that moment—so they didn't spell out the who and the when, as they would have in real life.)

A panel that focused only on commonly held information would choose Candidate A—one of the inferior candidates—reasoning that he had six attributes as opposed to Candidate B's four and Candidate C's three. A panel whose members broke free of groupthink and successfully shared information would realize that in fact Candidate C had all nine attributes and choose him instead.

Not surprisingly, panels that made no if-then plan chose the superior candidate only 18% of the time. Panels with if-then plans were much more likely to make the right decision, selecting the superior candidate 48% of the time.

PLAN FOR THE UNEXPECTED

If-then planning is particularly useful for dealing with the inevitable bumps in the road—the unforeseen complications, the minor (and major) disasters, those moments when confusion sets in. Studies show that people who decide in advance how they will deal with such snags are much more resilient and able to stay on track.

Begin by identifying potential risks, focusing on those that seem the most likely. If the new project management software you purchased turns out to be buggy or the new review process you've implemented is too cumbersome, what will you do? If a

Clinging to Lost Causes

Further studies by Wieber, Thürmer, and Gollwitzer show that if-then plans can help groups avoid another common problem: committing more and more resources to clearly failing projects. As the Nobel laureate Daniel Kahneman and his collaborator Amos Tversky pointed out decades ago, we tend to chase *sunk costs*—the time, effort, and money that we have put into something and can't get back out. It's irrational behavior. Once your team realizes that a project is failing, previous investments shouldn't matter. The best you can do is try to make smart choices with what you have left to invest. But too often we stay the course, unwilling to admit we have squandered resources that would have been better spent elsewhere. Groups, especially, tend to hang major supplier goes out of business or has a factory fire, will you have sufficient reserves on hand?

To create contingency if-then plans, you identify what action to take should one of those risks turn into a reality. Suppose your business unit is market testing two new product lines. Rather than assume that at least one of them will merit further investment, make an if-then plan that allows for a less optimistic outcome. For instance: "When we have third-quarter sales figures in hand, Carol will calculate ROI and build a business case for next-phase funding."

in there when it would be best to walk away, sometimes doubling down on their losing wagers. And the more cohesive they are, the greater the risk.

The dangers of identifying too much with one's team or organization are well documented: pressure to conform, for instance, and exclusion of atypical group members from leadership positions. When being a "good" team member is all that matters, groups often (implicitly or explicitly) discourage diverse ways of thinking, and they're loath to acknowledge their imperfections and errors of judgment. Hence the blind spot when it comes to sunk costs.

However, by taking the perspective of an independent observer, a group can gain the objectivity to scale back on its commitments to bad decisions or cut its losses altogether. In other words, by imagining that some other team made the initial investment, people free themselves up to do what's best in light of current circumstances, not previous outlays.

Wieber, Thürmer, and Gollwitzer hypothesized that if-then planning might be a particularly good tool for instilling this mind-set, for two reasons. First, studies showed that if-then plans helped individuals change strategies for pursuing goals, rather than continue with a failing approach. Second, additional research by Gollwitzer demonstrated that making if-then plans helped people take an outsider's view (they assumed the perspective of a physician when seeing blood in order to reduce feelings of disgust).

To test the effectiveness of if-then plans in scaling back group commitments, a study led by Wieber put subjects into teams of three and asked them to make joint investment decisions. Each team acted as a city council, deciding how much to invest in a public preschool project. During phase one, the groups received information casting the project in a very positive light, and they allocated funds accordingly. In phase two, they received both positive and negative information: Construction had begun and a local store was donating materials, but the building union wanted a substantial raise and environmental activists had voiced concerns about the safety of the land. Rationally, the teams should have begun to decrease funding at this point, given the uncertainty of the project's success. Finally, in phase three, the groups received mostly negative information: Oil had been found in the sand pit, parents were outraged, and fixing the problems would be time-consuming and expensive. Further scaling back was clearly called for.

So what did the teams do? Those that had made no if-then plans showed the typical pattern of commitment. They slightly increased the percentage of budget allocated to the project from phase one to phase three. In contrast, teams with if-then plans ("If we make a decision, we will take the perspective of a neutral observer that was not responsible for any prior investments") reduced their investments from phase one to phase three by 13%, on average.

When teams and organizations set goals, they tend to use sweeping, abstract language. But it's easier to frame your plans in if-then terms if you first break them down into smaller, more concrete subgoals and then identify the actions required to reach each subgoal. (See figure 26-1, "How to design if-then plans.") If you were trying to improve your team's communication, for example, you might set "Reduce information overload among staff members" as one subgoal. And after some brainstorming, you might decide to accomplish that by asking members who are forwarding any email to explain up front why they're doing so. (The rationale: People will be more selective about what they pass along if they have to provide a reason.) The if-then plan for each team member would be "If I forward any email, I'll include a brief note at the top describing what it is and why I'm sharing it." One manager I spoke with found that this if-then plan put an immediate end to the knee-jerk forwarding

FIGURE 26-1

How to design if-then plans

This flowchart shows how to translate a high-level ambition (in this instance, better communication) into detailed plans for execution

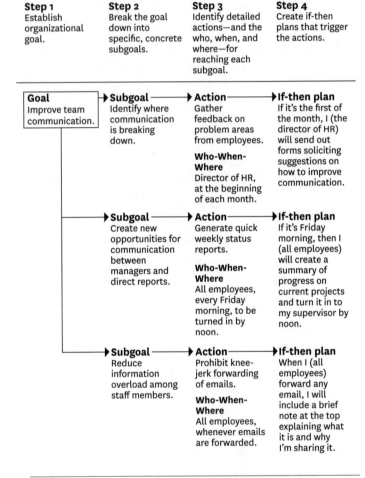

Step 1
Establish organizational goal.

Step 2
Break the goal down into specific, concrete subgoals.

Step 3
Identify detailed actions—and the who, when, and where—for reaching each subgoal.

Step 4
Create if-then plans that trigger the actions.

Goal Improve team communication.	**Subgoal** Identify where communication is breaking down.	**Action** Gather feedback on problem areas from employees. **Who-When-Where** Director of HR, at the beginning of each month.	**If-then plan** If it's the first of the month, I (the director of HR) will send out forms soliciting suggestions on how to improve communication.
	Subgoal Create new opportunities for communication between managers and direct reports.	**Action** Generate quick weekly status reports. **Who-When-Where** All employees, every Friday morning, to be turned in by noon.	**If-then plan** If it's Friday morning, then I (all employees) will create a summary of progress on current projects and turn it in to my supervisor by noon.
	Subgoal Reduce information overload among staff members.	**Action** Prohibit knee-jerk forwarding of emails. **Who-When-Where** All employees, whenever emails are forwarded.	**If-then plan** When I (all employees) forward any email, I will include a brief note at the top explaining what it is and why I'm sharing it.

that had clogged everyone's inbox with unnecessary information. It also increased the value of the emails that people did forward.

Specifying the who, when, and where is an ongoing process, not a onetime exercise. Ask team members to review their if-then plans regularly. Studies show that rehearsing the if-then link can more than double its effectiveness. It also allows groups to periodically reassess how realistic their plans are. Is anything harder or taking longer than expected? Are there steps that the team didn't plan for? If circumstances change, your if-then plans need to change, too—or they won't have the desired impact.

Though the research on if-then planning for teams and organizations is relatively new, the early results are promising, and social psychologists are examining several uses and benefits. (For instance, I'm studying whether it can be used to shift group mindsets from what I call "be good" thinking to "get better" thinking that fosters continuous improvement.) What's already becoming clear is that if-then planning helps groups frame their goals in a way that's achievable, providing a bridge between intentions and reality. It enables them to do more of what they mean to—and do it better—by fostering ownership and essentially reprogramming people to execute.

———

Heidi Grant, PhD, is Senior Scientist at the Neuroleadership Institute, and associate director for the Motivation Science Center at Columbia University. She is the author of the bestselling books *Nine Things Successful People Do Differently* (Harvard Business Review Press, 2012), *No One Understands You and What to Do About It* (Harvard Business Review Press, 2015), and *Reinforcements: How to Get People to Help You* (Harvard Busines Review Press, 2018). Follow her on Twitter @heidgrantphd.

Navigate Strategic Thinking Challenges

CHAPTER 27

When You Think the Strategy Is Wrong

by Amy Gallo

Chances are that at some point in your career you've been asked to implement a strategy that was developed by someone else. A manager's job is to execute that strategy, and to be sure that their team, unit, or department is aligned as well. But what if you believe the strategy you've been asked to implement is flawed? Perhaps you think the strategy won't achieve the intended result—or worse, that it will put the company at risk.

Adapted from "When You Think the Strategy Is Wrong" on hbr.org, February 4, 2010 (product #H004A5).

Regardless of the depth of your concern, you have an obligation to speak up. But immediately pressing the strategy panic button isn't always useful, and may brand you as an alarmist. It's important to find ways to express your concerns productively. By acting cautiously and thoughtfully, you can make your concerns heard while perhaps saving your team—or the company—time, energy, and money.

What the Experts Say

Strategy development is a difficult, time-intensive, and often messy process. The end result is never perfect. However, as a good citizen in any organization, you have an obligation to act if you see something wrong with your organization's strategy. Linda Hill, Harvard Business School professor and author of *Becoming a Manager*, says, "Anyone with a deep commitment to the organization owes it to that organization to ask questions and clear up confusions." However, you need to proceed cautiously. Don Sull, author of *The Upside of Turbulence*, cautions, "Saying 'this is stupid and wrong' isn't helpful." Before you cry "wrong strategy," follow these three steps to understand what is truly at stake and explore your motivations.

Step 1. Diagnose: Understand the full picture

An organization's strategy is often steeped in complex political issues. Before you speak up, try to understand the situation in which the strategy was developed. As Gary Neilson, executive adviser at the consulting firm Strategy&, points out, "Too many people view themselves as a self-appointed strategist for the company." Don't assume you know how or why the strategy was developed. Use your network to find out more about the process and the assumptions used. According to Hill, a good network will return useful information and advice if it includes a diverse set of people who have differing perspectives—what Hill calls, "a personal board of directors." Send out feelers to get more background about what went into the strategy and what its intended purpose is. Aim to find out what problem the company's leaders are trying to solve with the current strategy or if there is a shift in priorities that you don't know about. Gaining a perspective on what went into the strategy can help you to reflect on what is underlying your concerns.

Step 2. Reflect: Contextualize your concerns

When it comes to strategy, right or wrong is in the eye of the beholder. Sull points out that a "good enough strategy excellently implemented will trump a perfect strategy lukewarmly implemented nine times out of ten." Because no strategy is infallible, it's likely that there are things you feel should be different, but these things don't necessarily require you to cause a mutiny. Neilson urges that concerned employees ask themselves, "Is it that you would have expected a different direction or do you believe that the analysis, facts, or process that the company used [were] flawed?" It's your job to understand what about your unease is critical to raise and what is simply the result of a difference of opinion.

It's also important to ask yourself if you are using your objections as a reason not to do something difficult.

Sull says, "Middle managers may use imperfect strategy as an excuse not to take initiative." It may be that your unease is rooted in your resistance to change or resentment about not being included in the strategy development process. It's better to know the true source of your concerns before speaking up. After you've done your research and reflected on your motivations, if your concerns remain, it's time to verbalize them.

Step 3. Speak up: Proceed carefully

Start by going to your direct manager to share your apprehensions. Your manager may or may not have been involved in the development of the strategy, but they may know more about the background. This conversation should happen in private. Ask questions and enlist your manager's help in understanding why the company has chosen this strategy. You can use questions such as, "What are the assumptions behind the strategy?" "Could you explain to me why this particular piece is important?" or "What leeway do we have to adjust the strategy to the realities of the local market?"

It is important when sharing your concerns that you provide data that supports why you're raising questions in the first place. If you've done your research, you should have this information ready. You can make this conversation more successful by proposing alternative solutions that would help mitigate the risks you see. Don't accuse your manager or hold them responsible. Make it clear that you are not questioning their authority but trying to better understand the strategy you've been asked to implement.

When to let it go—and when not to

After taking the above steps, if your concerns have been shrugged off or disputed, you may need to choose your battles. "Skepticism is hugely helpful in organizations but bloody-minded obstinacy is not," Sull says. People have very little respect for someone who ruthlessly fights over imperfections. You may have to trust your boss or other superiors especially because there may be issues they are not at liberty to disclose. "In those cases, you may want to say, 'If you truly think this is the right direction, I will do it,'" Hill suggests.

Sull points out that there are rare cases where the strategy is putting the company at such risk that you may want to consider leaving the organization. These are cases where there are ethical concerns or the company may fail if the strategy is pursued in its current form. If faced with a strategy that is severely flawed or that you can't comfortably support, quitting may be the best option. And if you do leave, don't bury your concerns. Write a letter to the CEO, no matter where you are in the organization, explaining your decision and the risks you see in the strategy.

Principles to Remember

Do:

- Understand the root cause of your concerns

- Research the inputs and assumptions underlying the strategy

- Express your concerns to your immediate boss first

Don't:

- Insist that your concerns be heeded

- Assume you know the assumptions or reasoning behind the strategy

- Question the strategy in a public setting

Case Study: When the Competitive Advantage Is a Disadvantage

Laura Casela (some details, including her name, have been changed) joined a strategic communications firm started by two former consulting colleagues. Laura was brought in as the director of business development to help grow the year-old firm, and was excited about her new role and about the company's future. The firm was founded on a unique premise. Most communications firms rely on freelance writers to do a lot of their work, and clients have little knowledge about who these writers are. Laura's colleagues decided to change that by hiring stay-at-home moms who had left the industry to have more time with their families; they felt this was an untapped and experienced resource and, if leveraged appropriately, could be a competitive advantage for the young firm. The firm built its brand around this hiring approach and had success with it in its first year in the market.

However, soon after taking the job, Laura discovered that the leads she was pursuing were not converting into business. She was able to capture referrals, but when new leads went to the website, they seemed to lose interest. She asked a few would-be clients what turned them away and they explained they weren't looking for a business of stay-at-home moms. Many said it just didn't feel like "a right fit." Laura realized that "clients wanted the best writers they could get and they were hiring a communications firm to do the hiring for them. They didn't care who did the work, as long as the work was great."

Laura was conflicted; she believed in the brand and, like the founders, thought it would help the organization stand out in the crowded New York market. But the evidence showed something different. Laura shared what she learned with her colleagues and explained that despite how much she believed in the principle, this was an angle they should drop.

The founders were surprised, but they were open to what Laura had to say, primarily because of the evidence she provided, including client feedback and emails. Laura's speaking up had a huge impact, and the firm's founders, together with Laura, ended up working with a strategy consultant to rethink their branding.

———————

Amy Gallo is a contributing editor at *Harvard Business Review* and the author of the *HBR Guide to Dealing with Conflict* (Harvard Business Review Press, 2017). She writes and speaks about workplace dynamics. Follow her on Twitter @amyegallo.

CHAPTER 28

When Your Boss Gives You Conflicting Messages

by Len Schlesinger and Charlie Kiefer

Managers routinely give employees conflicting messages with respect to their objectives: "Be innovative" and "Follow established protocol." "Take risks" and "Don't expose the company to bad press." "Focus on the company's number-one initiative" and "All of these projects are a priority."

At an organizational level, conflicting goals can be conquered by a carefully set execution plan, as outlined

---

Adapted from "When Your Boss Gives You Conflicting Messages" on hbr.org, November 27, 2014 (product #H01QBD).

in chapter 18. But on an individual basis, navigating conflicting instructions can be both difficult and confusing. And while some managers may acknowledge the inconsistencies and ambiguities in these objectives, others may not. As an employee, how do you respond if your manager doesn't recognize the impossible position they've put you in?

People who find themselves in such a double bind have pretty predictable responses. Frustration and anger are most common. Less obvious reactions are the tendency to withdraw, shut down, and wait for clear direction that may never arrive. If you're feeling any of these reactions to your boss's requests, there's a good chance that a double bind is the cause. So, what can you do?

Don't Pretend the Conflict Doesn't Exist

When you're faced with priorities that are in direct conflict, it can be a natural instinct to just put your head down and try to get everything done. In his book *Flawed Advice and the Management Trap*, business theorist Chris Argyris describes the sequence of events that happens when individuals ignore tension between objectives: Organizations and their leaders craft messages that contain inconsistencies. They then make the problem worse by acting as if the messages are consistent— and they make it nearly impossible to resolve issues by labeling the inconsistent messages as "undiscussable."

It's not that you can't deal with conflicting messages; people do it all the time. But leaders put people in an impossible situation when they pretend that the messages don't conflict and preempt any discussion of the matter.

When this happens, you face a dilemma with two related consequences—one psychological and the other actual—that can be addressed separately.

Use humor

Dealing with the first consequence is straightforward. Remember, psychologically, the central problem is not the dilemma itself, but the fact that you can't confront it. So see it for what it is—a crazy-making situation. Be mindful of when it's affecting you. Laugh about it with friendly colleagues. Over time, you can remove many of the negative psychological aspects and ensure that the double bind doesn't play with your head. But it can, and perhaps should, still affect your behavior, so you must think strategically.

Discuss the undiscussable

Since the second consequence, undiscussability, is often one of the unwritten rules of the game, proceed with caution. Remember that the ultimate remedy is to make the organizational habit of undiscussability a topic of investigation and overt dialogue on the part of everyone in the system. It takes subtlety and time; going at it very directly early on can get you in deep trouble.

Start with a situation or dilemma that you immediately face. Talk to your manager about the bind you are in, and have them help you navigate that specific instance. Bring it up in a lighthearted way; for example: "OK, so I need to do something and not do it at the same time. Can you give me any insight or advice on how to pull that off? Or how to balance the two? Or trade them off? How have you navigated this kind of situation successfully in the past?" Helping you is your boss's job, and hopefully, to be a good coach.

Identify the Challenges and Move Forward

Regrettably, you may be met with "Of course we want you to do more, faster, with less. Grow up and get over it." Awareness of the reality you're facing is always a good thing, and at least you will have confirmed the challenges you face. There are two big ones that you need to consider:

1. What, specifically, can you do to be effective in this situation, when you're clearly being asked to do two contradictory things?

2. Can you figure out a way to make your boss more eager to help you?

To address the first challenge, you need to get as creative as you can, and then just do your best. Publicly building a strategy that attempts to manage through the contradictions with a positive spirit will likely provide an opportunity for your boss to be in a more active listening mode as you confront the inevitable issues.

For the second challenge, enroll your boss to support your efforts, even if they aren't instinctively eager to help. Explain why you're committed to this effort, and offer action items and tasks for your boss to contribute. Get them excited about investing in you. This enrollment is likely to be facilitated by your manager's belief that you are actively trying to succeed on the agenda as defined. Over time, they are likely to be more open to working with you to find ways to both navigate the conflicting messages and possibly bring awareness to the dysfunctional behavior.

Of course, there is no guarantee that this will work, but since you have released yourself from the psychological aspects of this issue through personal awareness, you will be able to play this game to the best of your ability. In the most severe cases, it may well be a game you simply choose not to play—by leaving the organization altogether.

———————

Len Schlesinger is Baker Foundation Professor of Business Administration at Harvard Business School. He previously served as the 12th president of Babson College and the Vice Chairman and Chief Operating Officer of Limited Brands (now L Brands). He is the coauthor of *What Great Service Leaders Know and Do*. **Charlie Kiefer** is founder of Innovation Associates, whose programs and services in insight, entrepreneurial thinking, and learning-based change permanently improve a large organization's ability to innovate. He has taught Corporate Entrepreneurship at the Sloan School of Management, MIT, and has coauthored a number of books and articles on entrepreneurship and insight. They are the coauthors, with Paul B. Brown, of *Just Start* (Harvard Business Review Press, 2012).

CHAPTER 29

When the Strategy Is Unclear, in Flux, or Always Changing

by Lisa Lai

It's one of the few facts in business everyone agrees on: *Without a clear and compelling strategy, your business will fail.* From MBA programs, to business book jackets, to the last keynote you attended, you've heard it repeated again and again.

Despite this, we frequently find ourselves managing in situations of strategic ambiguity—when it isn't clear where you're going or how you'll get there. Why does this happen? Market conditions shift rapidly. Customers have more choices than ever. Resources are constrained. Executives leave, interims are appointed, and searches drag on. The list continues, and even if your company is nimble enough to set strategy effectively at the top, keeping the entire organization strategically aligned is an entirely different challenge. Your company might have a clear strategic imperative, but your unit or team might not.

In my consulting practice, I work with leaders all over the world on strategy and execution, and they shift uncomfortably in their chairs every time I broach this topic. Strategic uncertainty can feel like slogging through mud. Leaders avoid investments. Decisions are deferred. Resources are frozen. Fear, uncertainty, and doubt drive bad behavior and personal agendas. Even so, companies often succeed or fail based on their managers' ability to move the organization forward precisely at times when the path ahead is hazy.

The best managers find ways to provide steady, realistic direction and to lead with excellence, even when the strategy isn't clear. Push your leaders for clarity, yes. In the meantime, be productive. There are three things you can do today that will put you in a better position to manage strategic ambiguity: Take pragmatic action, cultivate emotional steadiness, and tap into others' expertise.

Take Pragmatic Action

I'm a proponent of practical approaches to dealing with uncertainty. Doing something, anything, in support of your company's success makes you and your team feel better than doing nothing.

Get back to basics. Deliver value. First, focus on what you can control. You owe it to the organization and to your team to deliver value every day. What clientele does your team serve today and what do they expect or need from you? How can you perform better, faster, or smarter to deliver on the promise of excellent service? What matters to the organization's mission or vision? How can your team contribute to that? When uncertainty comes, first and foremost do good work. You'll put the company in the best possible position to navigate new strategic choices.

Place intelligent bets. What's likely? When the strategy is uncertain, the best managers acknowledge what's unknown, but also look ahead to what *is* known and what is *likely* to happen. What do you know about the dynamics impacting your company? What options are being discussed? What does your boss think will happen? What can you do today to prepare yourself, your team, and potentially your clients for change? In almost every case, managers can place intelligent bets and start to work toward a future state—even when the complete landscape remains out of focus.

Operate in sprints: Embrace short-term strategies. Once you've focused your team on delivering value and started to explore what's possible, you're prepared to move forward with a discrete set of priorities. Take a note from organizations that use agile methods and create your own strategic sprint. What can you do personally to contribute to strategic clarity for your part of the business?

What projects can your team execute in 30, 60, or 90 days that will benefit the organization regardless of which direction the strategy takes? Strategy isn't only the work of senior executives—any work you do to further the company's capabilities and position your team for the future is a great investment. Don't stand still, awaiting the "final" answer on strategy. Move your team and the company forward.

Cultivate Emotional Steadiness

Strategic ambiguity pushes you out of your comfort zone. When there's clear, unwavering direction, you can focus on defined targets and deliver results. When strategies shift, or are hinting toward a shift, it's normal to feel unsettled, and you'll see this in your team too. Here are three steps you can take to help yourself and your team navigate the emotions of strategic ambiguity.

Be proactive. Learn more. One of the reasons I suggest pragmatic action is because doing something concrete helps you move beyond your raw emotions. But there's more to emotional steadiness. Questions arise naturally: How will this impact my group? What if everything we're doing today alters? What if this involves job changes, layoffs, or lost resources? Learn as much as you can so you're informed, not just reacting to rumor and innuendo. Use your internal network and ask others in the organization for insight, context, and clarity. When you've done the hard work of sense-making, you'll be able to anticipate the questions your team will ask and prepare the most effective answers you can.

Acknowledge and navigate emotions. Emotional steadiness requires that you be intentional about the way you show up in the workplace. Your role is to be calm, transparent, and steady, all while painting a vision for the future. Acknowledge your emotions and talk to a peer or your boss if you need to work through them. Play out the worst-case scenario in your mind and then move on to the more likely outcome. Chances are the reality isn't as bad as what you might conjure up when your emotions are heightened. Commit to avoiding stress responses, frustration, rumors, or other nonproductive behavior. Your team members are watching and taking their cues from you.

Keep team communication open. Strategic uncertainty can cause managers to communicate with team members less frequently and less openly. "If I don't have clarity to provide, why not wait?" the thinking goes. But in truth, ambiguous situations require you to communicate even more than normal. To demonstrate emotional steadiness, share your own emotions and acknowledge those of your team in productive ways. Let team members know that what they feel is okay. But talk with them about your commitment to being emotionally steady even during times of uncertainty. Ask them to do the same and come to you if they are frustrated or concerned. Maintaining open dialogue will keep your team engaged and aligned until a clear direction emerges.

Tap into Others' Expertise

Leading through periods of uncertainty and change can be isolating for managers. Remind yourself that you are not alone. You have a network of people who have likely faced similar challenges and you can tap into their experiences. Here are three ways you can tap into the expertise of others for support.

Imagine your most respected leader's approach. What would they do in your situation? How would they handle the ambiguity or state of flux? How would they view the way you're handling yourself? This exercise can be incredibly powerful in helping you stay calm and emotionally steady, exercise your critical thinking, and take pragmatic action even in the most uncertain circumstances. Those we most respect have demonstrated traits we admire. Tap into their strengths to inform your own.

Engage other managers. Managers often believe they need to "be strong" and go it alone to demonstrate managerial confidence and competency. That's not true. My executive clients reach out to peers and former colleagues regularly for advice, counsel, and emotional support. If someone you know reached out to you to ask for your advice, you'd happily provide support and feel valued as a peer. Your network will feel the same. Start the conversation with "I could really use another point of view" and you'll be surprised how quickly others engage.

Embrace the wisdom of thought leaders. Your network becomes global when you expand beyond those you know personally to those you can access in today's digital environment. The greater your understanding of how others think about strategic agility and change leadership, the better you'll be able to navigate ambiguity in your company. The brightest and most inspiring minds are at your fingertips—read books and articles, listen to podcasts and interviews, and watch instructive videos, webinars, and more to expand your thinking and learn new approaches relevant to your specific situation.

The ability to thrive during periods of strategic uncertainty separates the great managers who go on to become exceptional leaders from the rest. Don't allow a lack of clarity at your company to cast a shadow over your confidence or performance. Even in the most challenging and ambiguous of situations, you put yourself in a position to succeed when you commit to taking pragmatic action while demonstrating emotional steadiness and drawing on the expertise of others.

———————

Lisa Lai is an adviser, consultant, and coach for some of the world's most successful leaders and companies. She is also a moderator of global leadership development programs for Harvard Business School Publishing. Find her on Facebook, visit her website at www.laiventures .com, or follow her on Twitter @soul4breakfast.

Questions to Inspire Strategic Thinking

To be an effective strategic thinker, you must regularly ask questions—both of yourself and others—to better understand how your work fits into your company's big-picture objectives and the competitive forces in your industry. The following questions are drawn from the chapters of this book and are grouped together according to specific situations or problems you may face. By regularly referring to this list, you'll be able to see challenges from new angles and shape your work to maximize your contribution while better aligning your team with organizational goals.

Understand Your Organization's Strategy

What's our strategy—and my role in executing it?

Reflect on these questions yourself and reach out to others in your organization—including your boss, peers, and employees—to better understand your company's strategic objectives.

- What are the company's major strategic objectives right now?

- What is our company already great at?

- What are the major needs, challenges, and opportunities we're facing over the next six months? Year? In the long term?

- How does my team fit into this picture?

- What are the top priorities for my group? What are the big needs, challenges, and opportunities that we should tackle in the next six months? Year? In the long term?

- What role should I play in carrying out this strategy?

- What are the major needs, challenges, and opportunities I should take on in the next six months? Year? In the long term?

- What are my boss's and colleagues' major objectives right now within the organization? How can I support them?

- What is the strategic intent of the leaders at the level above mine?

- What are the key choices that I make in my jurisdiction?

- With what strategic logic can I align those choices with those above me?

- How can I communicate the logic of my strategy choices to those who report to me?

What are the risks to our strategy—and to me?

Considering strategic objectives, ask yourself where the biggest risks are for your team and your own professional life.

- What are the major sources of uncertainty in my team's future?

- What are the external risks (for example, funding, competition with other units, potential reorganization)?

- What are the internal risks (for example, personnel changes, team dynamics, office politics)?

- What are the major sources of uncertainty in my own future?

- What are the professional risks to my success (for example, professional goals; experience, training, and accreditation; work logistics)?

- What are the personal risks to my success (for example, health, family, finances)?

Develop a Big-Picture Perspective

What is the purpose and role of my organization?

Reflect on these questions regularly, so you're keeping organizational priorities front of mind.

- Why does the organization exist, and what is its purpose?

- If the organization didn't exist, what difference would it make to the world? What would be missing?

- What does the organization offer our customers—and what does it *not*? How and why does this offering deliver value to these customers?

- What does this offering produce for the business and for shareholders?

- How do the people within the organization behave—toward customers, other stakeholders, and each other?

Who are my organization's key stakeholders?

Brainstorm a list of people your company serves. Then answer these questions about each one to narrow down your list into a focused group of stakeholders.

- Does the stakeholder have a fundamental impact on the organization's performance? *(Required response: Yes)*

- Can we clearly identify what we want from the stakeholder? *(Required response: Yes)*

- Is the relationship dynamic—that is, do we want it to grow? *(Required response: Yes)*

- Can the organization exist without or easily replace the stakeholder? *(Required response: No)*

- Has the stakeholder already been identified through another relationship? *(Required response: No)*

Where are opportunities for change in my organization?

Interview or survey your colleagues to better understand their fundamental beliefs and assumptions about your company's current situation. Use their answers to identify areas that could be changed.

- What are some key assumptions inherent in your day-to-day activities—the established "rules" under which the organization generally operates? What core values are "givens"?

- What are some of your own beliefs about the organization? What makes it perform effectively at present? In what areas does the organization devote too much—or too little—time and resources?

- What is the organization's competitive space? Are there ways it might be redefined?

What trends are happening inside my company?

Use these questions about your company's people, processes, products, and strategy to note any early signals of change.

- Have there been any new hires or departures of key employees in the company? Has there been an increase in external hires?

- Have there been important changes in relationships and power dynamics that could impact my and my team's efforts?

- Are my employees engaged? How might that impact the speed and quality of my and my department's initiatives?

- What key process or technology changes are occurring in other departments?

- Are there patterns in the types of requests I am receiving from key stakeholders? What might these requests signal?

- Has my team experienced a change in the service they receive from internal colleagues?

- How might the introduction of a new product, service, or geography by my company impact my line of business? Does a series of new products signal a change in direction?

- Are there signals that a drop in sales of a key product might be due to internal factors?

- Does a series of acquisitions signal a new direction for the organization?

- Are there changes in resource allocation across the company?

- Are there signals that stakeholder priorities have changed?

- Given all these trends, what do these changes signal for my department or my own work?

Align Decisions with Strategic Objectives

How do I make a strategic decision?

When faced with a tough issue or problem, the following questions will help you understand the impact of your choice.

- What preexisting company goals or priorities will be affected by the decision?

- What are realistic alternatives to the choice I'm facing?

- What are the pros and cons of each alternative?

- What important information am I missing?

- What are the potential short- and long-term ramifications of my choice? What impact will my decision have one year in the future?

- What perspectives should I consider from stakeholders? What cross-functional considerations should I take into account?

- What trade-offs seem most appropriate to make in this situation?

- Why and how much does the team support my decision?

- *(One to two months in the future)* How did this decision pan out? Where should I make corrections, and what can I learn from what's happened?

Set Priorities and Manage Trade-Offs

How do I create a plan to execute multiple goals?

When organizational goals don't mesh, define a way to meet them by asking these questions.

- Can I work on all of the strategic goals at the same time? If not, what do I need to tackle first?

- Are there resources or knowledge that can be gained from an early opportunity that could help another objective later?

- How much can I and my team do at once? Do we have the resources to focus on more than one major strategic project at a time?

- What will it take to keep the current business going while we are driving new strategic initiatives?

- Do I have people in place that have the skills and know-how to move into new strategic territory?

- Will I need to hire new people or train existing staff? What's the extent of this investment, and how will it be integrated with the current team?

- If the market or our resources change during planning, should our original assumptions about how to compete still prevail?

- Have our investigations suggested specific learnings that would substantially alter those assumptions?

- Are there serious disagreements between key stakeholders about executing the strategy? What's the root cause of the opposition?

- Are skeptical colleagues raising legitimate concerns that might call for refashioning the way forward?

Align Your Team Around Strategy Goals

What key objectives should my team be focusing on?

Define your most important work with your team and align them toward it.

- Will success in this outcome drive the mission of the larger organization?

- Is it supporting, and supported by, our primary business goals?

- Will achieving it make a statement to the organization about what's most important?

- Will it lead to the execution of our strategy?

- Is it the appropriate stretch?

- Are we excited about it? Do we have an emotional connection to it?

How can I inspire strategic thinking in my team?

Ask your team these questions to drive clarity, alignment, and strategic insight.

- What are we doing today?

- Why are we doing the work we're doing? Why now?

- How does what we're doing today align with the bigger picture?

- What does success look like for our team?

- What else could we do to achieve more, better, faster?

- How are we doing things differently than our competitors?

- What methods should we use to find out more about industry trends and innovations?

How do I communicate a vision to my team?

When the strategy changes, carefully consider how you'll communicate the change by thinking about each of these questions.

- What does my team care most about? What do they know about the current status of our project, goal, or bigger strategy? How do they feel about the team and organization right now, and what are they expecting?

- How is the vision relevant to them? How would they challenge the vision? What would make them resistant?

- What are specific, measurable goals and deadlines? How can I help my team achieve them?

- How will they benefit in the end? What problems am I trying to solve that will make their lives better in some way?

Organizational Strategy: A Primer

This guide has focused on the day-to-day aspects of strategic thinking—understanding your company's objectives, setting priorities, and aligning your team—and has mostly taken as a given that your company already has a clear and defined strategy.

However, the further you advance in your career, the more you'll be a participant in *developing* your company's strategy. And even if you're a new or midlevel manager now, understanding how and why your leaders set the organizational strategy will help you execute it with your team.

This appendix explains what strategy *is*, how to formulate it, and what leaders should be thinking about when they set and update company strategy.

Adapted from *Harvard Business Review Manager's Handbook* (product #10004), Harvard Business Review Press, 2017.

What Is Strategy?

Bruce Henderson, founder of Boston Consulting Group, wrote that "strategy is a deliberate search for a plan of action that will develop a business's competitive advantage and compound it." Competitive advantage, he continued, is found in differences: "The differences between you and your competitors are the basis of your advantage." Henderson believes that no two competitors can coexist if they seek to do business in the same way. They must differentiate themselves to survive.

For example, two men's clothing stores on the same block—one featuring formal attire and the other focusing on leisure wear—can potentially prosper. But if the two stores sell the same things under the same terms, one or the other will perish. More likely, the one that differentiates itself through price, product mix, or ambiance will survive. Harvard Business School professor Michael Porter, whose work inspires modern corporate strategy, concurs: "Competitive strategy is about being different. It means deliberately choosing a different set of activities to deliver a unique mix of value." Consider these examples:

- Southwest Airlines didn't become the most profitable air carrier in North America by copying its rivals. It differentiated itself with a strategy of low fares, frequent departures, point-to-point service, and customer-pleasing service.

- Toyota's strategy in developing the hybrid-engine Prius car was to create competitive advantage within two important customer segments: People who want a vehicle that is environmentally benign and cheap to operate, and those who covet the latest thing in auto engineering. The company also hoped that the learning associated with the Prius would give it leadership in a technology with huge *future potential.*

Strategies may center on low-cost leadership, technical uniqueness, or focus. Porter also argues that you can think about them in terms of strategic position, "performing *different* activities from rivals' or performing similar activities in *different* ways." These positions emerge from three, sometimes overlapping sources:

- **Need-based positioning.** Companies that follow this approach aim to serve all or most of the needs of an identifiable set of customers. These customers may be price sensitive, demand a high level of personal attention and service, or may want products or services that are uniquely tailored to their needs. Target's focus on image-conscious shoppers is an example of this type of positioning.

- **Variety-based positioning.** Here, a company chooses a narrow subset of product/service offerings from within the wider set offered in the industry. It can succeed with this strategy if it delivers faster, better, or at a lower cost than competitors. Walmart's past decision not to stock big-ticket items like appliances and electronics is an example of this type of positioning.

- **Access-based positioning.** Some strategies can be based around access to customers. A discount merchandise chain, for example, may choose to locate its stores exclusively in low-income neighborhoods. This reduces competition from suburban shopping malls and provides easy access for its target market of low-income shoppers, many of whom don't have automobiles. Target's decision to locate stores in urban environments is an example of this type of positioning.

Simply being different, of course, won't keep you in business. Your strategy must also deliver value. And customers define value in different ways: Lower cost, greater convenience, greater reliability, faster delivery, more aesthetic appeal, easier use. The list of customer-pleasing values is extremely long. As you evaluate your own company's strategy for gaining competitive advantage, ask yourself these questions:

- Do we differentiate ourselves based on need, variety, or access?

- How does our positioning attract customers away from rivals? How does it draw new customers into the market?

- What value does our strategy aim to provide? Does it deliver?

- What tangible advantage does this strategy provide for our company?

Understanding your company's approach here will hone your ability to think strategically. And it will also allow you to formulate your own group's strategy from the ground up.

Developing Strategy

If you haven't had much experience developing strategy, know that most managers are in the same position. That's because it isn't an everyday activity. "Executives hone their management capabilities by tackling problems over and over again," notes Harvard Business School professor Clayton Christensen. "Changing strategy, however, is not usually a task that managers face repeatedly. Once companies have found a strategy that works, they want to use it, not change it. Consequently, most management teams do not develop a competence in strategic thinking."

Whether you're revitalizing your team's business model or building a new business unit from scratch, you need to analyze how your company's external circumstances relate to its internal resources. That's the essence of strategy building: finding unique links between the opportunities and threats that present themselves to your business and your particular capacity to respond.

The order in which you perform this analysis is important. It yields the best results when you begin by identifying a problem out in the world, then work toward a solution inside your company. The process rarely succeeds in the opposite direction: A strategic initiative that's not grounded in a real business need is likely to make you *less* competitive rather than more.

Over the past few decades, many frameworks for building strategy have emerged, from the work of Porter and others. The following steps are a generalized outline of these processes, which may prepare you to contribute to your company's strategy, as well as ensure your team's plans are well constructed.

Step 1: Look outside to identify threats and opportunities

There are always threats in your organization's outer environment: new entrants, demographic changes, suppliers who might cut you off, substitute products that could undermine your business, and macroeconomic trends that may reduce the ability of your customers to pay. Opportunity also lurks in a new-to-the-world technology, an unserved market, and so forth.

Deepen your understanding of this landscape by gathering the views of customers, suppliers, and industry experts you may interact with in your role. Have conversations with others in the organization to identify current threats and opportunities. Some firms, particularly in technological fields, enlist teams of scientists and engineers to analyze markets, competitors, and technical developments. It's their job to look for anything that could threaten their current business or point toward new directions that their business should follow. Gain exposure to this work if possible.

Whether you're contributing directly to strategy development in your role or simply trying to understand the environment in which you operate, consider the following questions:

- What is the economic environment in which we must operate? How is it changing?

- What will our customers want/expect from us in 5 to 10 years? How will the world have changed?

- What major threats do we face now or are we likely to face soon? What aspects of the current environment are our competitors struggling to adapt to?

- What opportunities for profitable action lay before us? What are the risks associated with different opportunities and potential courses of action?

Step 2: Look inside at resources, capabilities, and practices

Internal resources and capabilities can either frame and support or constrain your company's strategy, especially for a larger company with many employees and fixed assets. And rightly so. A strategy to exploit an unserved market in the electronics industry might not be feasible if your firm lacks the financial capital and human knowledge to carry it off. Likewise, a strategy that requires entrepreneurialism from your employees probably won't get off the ground if your company's management practices reward years of service over individual performance.

These internal capabilities—especially the human ones—matter greatly, but strategists often overlook them. To whatever degree you participate in organizational or team strategy development, consider questions like:

- What are our competencies as an organization or team? How do these give us an advantage relative to competitors?

- What resources support or limit our actions?

- What attitudes and behaviors do our employment practices encourage?

- What is our workforce good at, and what does it struggle to accomplish?

- What does it take to implement real change here?

Step 3: Consider strategies for change

Once you have a picture of how the changing external world affects your business and what the company or your team looks like right now from the inside, it's time to think about directions for change. Christensen has advocated that strategy teams first prioritize the threats and opportunities they find (he calls them "driving forces" of competition) and then discuss each one in broad strokes. Like all idea-generation sessions, these conversations will be most successful if you push your team to create many alternatives. There is seldom one way to do things, and in some cases, the best parts of two different strategies can be combined to make a stronger, third option.

As you're working with your boss, your peers, or your own team, don't be too attached to your new ideas at this stage. Check your facts and question your assumptions. Some information is bound to be missing, so determine where your knowledge gaps are and how to fill them. As your options start to take shape, vet the leading strategy choices with others, including longtime employees, subject-matter experts, and other industry players in your network. (You'll have to be careful how much information you share with each person, of course.) Collecting a wide range of reactions will help you counter groupthink.

Step 4: Build a good fit among strategy-supporting activities

Good business strategies, according to Porter, *combine* activities into a chain whose links are mutually supporting and lock out imitators. Take the rise of Southwest Airlines as an example: As Porter describes, the company's breakthrough strategy was based on rapid gate turnaround that allowed Southwest to make frequent departures and get the most out of its expensive aircraft assets. The emphasis on gate turnaround also dovetailed with the low-cost, high-convenience proposition the airline offered its customers. Critical activities across the company's operations supported these goals: the highly motivated and effective gate personnel and ground crews, a no-meals policy, and no interline baggage transfers. All made rapid turnarounds possible. "Southwest's strategy," wrote Porter, "involves a whole system of activities, not a collection of parts. Its competitive advantage comes from the way its activities fit and reinforce each other."

To systematize the strategy in your own organization, focus on these issues:

- What activities and processes are involved in carrying out our strategy? Which are most (and least) important to the success of the strategy?

- How could we modify each activity and process to better support the strategy? How can we organize these changes to compound our advantages?

- What resources and constraints should we plan for? How will we implement the highest-priority and highest-impact changes?

Step 5: Create alignment

Once you've developed a satisfactory strategy, your job is only half done. The other half is implementation. You'll need to create alignment between your people and operations, and your strategy. This is critical for managers at any level. Ideally, employees at every level in your company will understand (1) what the strategy is; (2) what their role is in making it work; and (3) what the benefits of the strategy will be to the organization and to them as individuals. Only when your people have a strong grasp of all three points will they be able—and willing—to carry out their work.

Managers like you play two roles in this process. As a *coordinator*, you must organize work in your department so that those everyday efforts support the business's strategic intentions. That means drafting assignments, streamlining processes, and reshaping roles so that no one's time is wasted and everyone feels connected to the shared sense of purpose. And as a *communicator*, you must help people understand the strategy and how their jobs contribute to it. Even your entry-level employees should be able to articulate the goals of the organization and explain how their efforts every day fit in.

Index